Touring China
漫 游 神 州

Touring China

Index

漫游神州

目　次

Touring China
漫游神州

FOREIGN LANGUAGES PRESS   BEIJING

外文出版社·北京

Sketch Map of China
游览示意图

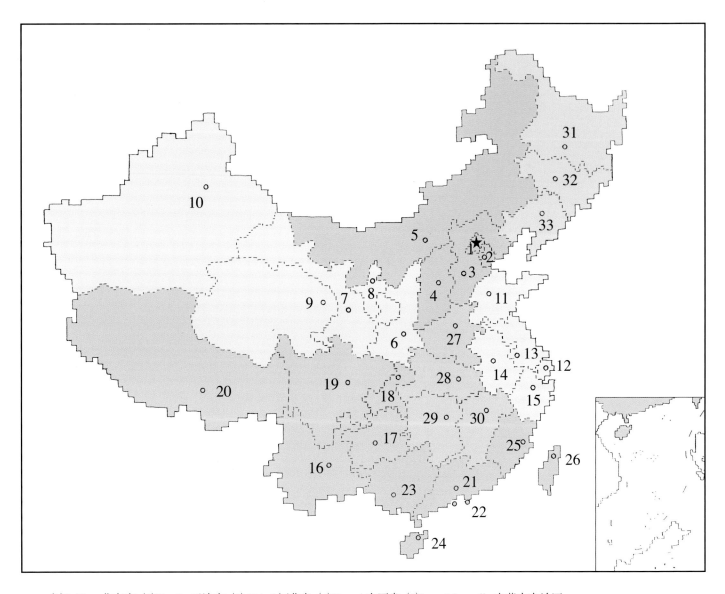

(1)Beijing 北京市、(2)Tianjin 天津市、(3) Hebei 河北省、(4)Shanxi 山西省、(5)Inner Mongolia 内蒙古自治区。

(6)Shaanxi 陕西省、(7)Gansu 甘肃省、(8)Ningxia 宁夏回族自治区、(9)Qinghai 青海省、(10)Xinjiang 新疆维吾尔自治区。

(11)Shandong 山东省、(12)Shanghai 上海市、(13)Jiangsu 江苏省、(14)Anhui 安徽省、(15)Zhejiang 浙江省。

(16)Yunnan 云南省、(17)Guizhou 贵州省、(18)Chongqing 重庆市、(19)Sichuan 四川省、(20)Tibet 西藏自治区。

(21)Guangdong 广东省、(22)Hong Kong 香港特别行政区、(23)Guangxi 广西壮族自治区、(24)Hainan 海南省、(25)Fujian 福建省、

(26)Taiwan 台湾省、(27)Henan 河南省、(28)Hubei 湖北省、(29)Hunan 湖南省、(30)Jiangxi 江西省。

(31)Heilongjiang 黑龙江省、(32)Jilin 吉林省、(33)Liaoning 辽宁省。

Preface

China is a vast country with beautiful scenery, 5,000 years of brilliant history and a wealth of cultural relics. If you have the chance to visit China, you will feel the charm of its ancient civilization.

There are many wonders in China, and the Great Wall is one of them. According to historical records, the earliest Great Wall emerged in the 7th century BC. From the Spring and Autumn Period (770-476 BC) to the 16th century, there were 20 dynasties that were involved in the construction of the Great Wall. The greatest projects included the Qin Great Wall, built by Emperor Qin Shi Huang (reigned between 246 and 209 BC), the Han Great Wall built by Emperor Wudi (reigned between 140 and 87 BC), and the Ming Great Wall built by Emperor Taizu (reigned between 1368 and 1399). The garrisoned cities, passes, beacon towers and tunnels form a complete military protection system. Long walls and countless watchtowers were built according to the geographic situation of the mountains. The dragon-like Great Wall is the symbol of the hardships of the ancient people and the wisdom of our ancestors.

Grotto art is another wonder with a long history. The famous grottoes are the ones at Dunhuang, Yungang and Longmen. The Dunhuang Grottoes, which were first carved in the year 366, number 492, with over 1,000 niches, 2,415 colored sculptures and 45,000 square meters of mural paintings. The Yungang Grottoes were first carved in 453, with 53 niches and 51,000 statues. The Longmen Grottoes were carved after Emperor Xiaowen (reigned between 471 and 500) moved his capital to Luoyang, in Henan Province. There are 2,100 niches and 100,000 statues. Besides, there are dozens of grottoes scattered on the Maiji Mountain, at the Bingling Temple, on the Tianlong Mountain and at Dazu, with countless statues. The common characteristics of these grottoes are that they are all carved on cliffs, and the statues of Buddha are carved in a simple way with smooth lines, beautiful postures, and vivid body language. The contents of many grottoes are like TV series, depicting China's long history and brilliant culture vividly. These grottoes attract millions of people to explore their art and pursue the mystery of China's ancient civilization.

Tombs of emperors are a rare wonder as well. The earliest one is the tomb of the Yellow Emperor. The tombs of Emperor Qin Shi Huang, Emperor Wudi of the Han Dynasty, Emperor Taizong of the Tang Dynasty, Emperor Taizu of the Song Dynasty, the 13 tombs of the Ming Dynasty, and the East and the West tombs of the Qing Dynasty all took tremendous amounts of human and financial resources. Among the tombs excavated so far, the mausoleum containing the terracotta army of Emperor Qin Shi Huang is the largest in scale. According to historical records, he started the construction of his tomb soon after he took the throne. The mausoleum took 37 years and 700,000 laborers to complete. There are palaces, rows of officials and military arrays in the mausoleum, indicating the emperor's courage and insight to unify China. The Ming Tombs near Beijing were constructed for the 13 emperors of the Ming Dynasty. So far, only the Dingling Tomb of the 14th emperor and his two empresses has been excavated. There were 26 boxes filled with over 3,000 pieces of jewelry and jade wares found in it. It is virtually an underground palace.

The most representative cultural relics in China are palaces. Palaces are the most significant part of China's architectural art. In history, emperors constructed their palaces immediately after they came to the throne. Emperor Qin Shi Huang constructed the Epang Palace, that covered an area of 150 kilometers, and it still had not been completed when the dynasty fell. It is said that the fire that destroyed it lasted for three months. It is estimated that the Hanyuan Hall and Linde Hall in the Daming Palace of the Tang Dynasty (618-907), now in ruins, were as magnificent as the Hall of Great Harmony in Beijing's Forbidden City. According to Tang Dynasty illustrations, the palaces were like fairy towers. The Changle Palace, Weiyang Palace and Changxin Palace of the Han Dynasty were all famous palace complexes in Chinese history. However, they were all destroyed during upheavals. The most complete and magnificent classic buildings preserved so far are the Forbidden City in Beijing, the Forbidden City in Shenyang, the Ligong Palace in Chengde and the Potala Palace in Tibet. They are all imposing, luxurious, and magnificent, with splendid halls, towers, and pavilions. The original structures still remain, although they have been renovated several times.

Gardens fall into the category of cultural relics as well. They are divided into imperial and official gardens. Imperial gardens are large and magnificent, with real mountains and rivers in the background, such as Beihai Park, Summer Palace and Yuanmingyuan (Old Summer Palace) in Beijing, and the Summer Resort in Chengde, with green mountains, blue rivers, green trees, and pagodas and halls. Official gardens are exquisitely structured with artificial hills and streams. There are many in Suzhou, Hangzhou, Wuxi and Yangzhou. Their elegance comes from making full use of trees, hills, lakes and stones.

Buddhist holy sites have an important position in Chinese architectural history. They are famous for their unique designs, and primitive and simple styles. The most representative ones are Mount Wutai, Mount Putuo, Mount Jiuhua and Mount Emei. There are 47 temples preserved on Mount Wutai. Although Xiantong, Zhenhai, Nanshan and Longquan temples on Mount Wutai are magnificent, their original aspects have been lost due to constant renovations. However, the Nanchan Temple and Light of Buddhism Temple preserve the styles of the Tang Dynasty. Mount Putuo has the most temples of any area in China, the biggest being Puji, Fayu and Huiji temples. The temples on Mount Jiuhua, known as a "Buddhist Kingdom," are the largest in scale. At one time, there were 300 temples and 4,000 monks there. Huacheng Temple and Diyuan Temple still attract many disciples. Mount Emei was first sacred to Taoism, and later became sacred to Buddhism, with 100 big and small temples. Of them, Wannian Temple and Baoguo Temple are the biggest. All the Buddha statues in the halls are gilded. White Horse Temple, Hanshan Temple, Shaolin Temple and Hanging Temple all display the essence of ancient Chinese architecture.

Buddhist and Taoist temples are scattered all over China. Mount Taishan in the east, Mount Huashan in the west, Mount Hengshan in the south, Mount Hengshan (in different handwriting from the former one) in the north and Mount Songshan in the center preserve colorful cultural relics and are set in beautiful natural scenery. The Bixia Ancestral Hall is huge and is divided into two courtyards. The Temple of the Jade Emperor was constructed on the top of Mount Taishan. Its simple, primitive and magnificent buildings are rare in China. The Zhenyue Palace on Mount Huashan is located between Fairy Peak and Lotus Peak, surrounded with pine trees, serving as an ideal place for cultivation. The statue of the Jade Emperor was worshiped in the Central Hall. The

Nantai, Jingtu, Hanging and Fuyan temples are on Mount Hengshan in the south. Zhurong Temple is built on a cliff, with the blue sky above and a valley underneath. Its 40 halls contain over 80 statues of Buddha. The two big halls, in the north and in the south, are linked by a plank road. Songyue Temple and Shaolin Temple, with red walls and yellow tiles, on Mount Songshan are magnificent. Some temples are located in front of hills, some are hanging, some are set among pine trees and some are on top of hills.

Exotic mountains and precipitous hills are major components of natural scenery in China. The well-known Mount Huangshan has hundreds of valleys and peaks, and "sea of clouds" coats it frequently. When exotic pine trees, grotesque rocks and the "sea of clouds" are in harmony, the scenery is breathtaking. The Wulingyuan Nature Reserve is a rare natural scenic spot, in which the highlights are the Zhangjiajie Nature Reserve, Tianzi Mountain and Huang's Family Village. Over 2,000 peaks, like stone bamboos, rear their heads in an area of 800 square kilometers. The place is also famous for its green trees, and rare wildlife. The Stone Forest in Yunnan Province is a unique sight, covering an area of 26,800 hectares. There are over a dozen scenic spots including the Greater Stone Forest, Lesser Stone Forest, Lion Hill, Purple Cloud Cave, Stone Forest Lake and Sharp Peak Pond. The exotic stones and rocks look like forests when seen from afar.

Rivers, lakes and seas are works of nature. On the Yangtze River, traversing China from west to east, the most magnificent scenery is found at the Three Gorges — Qutang, Wuxia and Xiling. The Yellow River is the symbol of the Chinese nation. Its Hukou Waterfall thunders in the valley. The Lijiang River in the Guangxi Zhuang Autonomous Region has world-famous natural scenery. The Jiuzhaigou Nature Reserve is surrounded by snow-capped mountains, deep valleys, primitive forests, and 100 lakes and waterfalls.

Forests, plains, desserts and islands are other components of the scenery in China. Green bamboos in southern China, white birch trees in the Changbai Mountains, poplar trees in Xinjiang, primitive forests in the Greater Hinggan Mountains are like nature's own pictures. The Western Liaoning, Central North China, Shandong and Western Sichuan plains are the four largest plains in China. Of the deserts located in northwestern China, the Taklimakan is the biggest one, and is famous for its huge dunes. China's islands are countless. The Zhoushan Archipelago look like pieces of green jade scattered and shining in the sea.

Touring China is an album with beautiful pictures and explanatory text, introducing China's history and natural scenery. It is both erudite and readable, with high artistic and appreciation value.

前　言

中国，幅员辽阔，风景壮丽，有悠久的光辉历史，有珍贵的文物古迹，是一个具有五千年灿烂文化的国家。倘若您有机会来中国观光旅游，您会感受到中华文明的魅力并获得美的享受。

漫游神州 胜读万卷史书

在中国有许许多多的人间奇迹，载入了世界文化的历史史册，万里长城就是其中的一页。据载，最早出现的长城，大约在公元前七世纪前后，距今已有二千六百年之久。从春秋战国时期至公元十六世纪止，先后有二十多个王朝和诸候参与修筑长城。其中工程最大的是秦始皇（前246-209在位）修筑的秦长城、汉武帝（前140-87在位）修筑的汉长城、明太祖（1368-1399在位）修筑的明长城。那些著名的镇城、路城、营城、关口、烽燧、战道等雄关要塞，构成了一个完整的军事防御体系。绵延万里的墙体，数不胜数的敌楼，随山而建，形成了千变万化的建筑风貌。这势若游龙的长城，光辉灿烂的业迹，向后人展示着中国劳动人民的千辛万苦，铭刻着世代祖辈的聪明智慧。每当我们看到它便浮想联翩，百感交集，似乎又看到了硝烟弥漫的战火，骏马嘶鸣的疆场。

石窟艺术是中国历史上的又一奇迹，它就像一部古老的史记，记载了中国的漫长岁月。著名的敦煌、云冈、龙门以及其他众多石窟，令人赞叹不已。敦煌石窟，开创于前秦建元二年（366），现存洞窟四百九十二个，窟室千余龛，彩塑二千四百一十五尊，壁画四万五千多平方米。云冈石窟，开创于北魏兴安二年（453），窟室五十三个，造像五万一千余尊。然后，北魏孝文帝（471-500在位），迁都洛阳，龙门石窟相继开凿。建成窟室二千一百多个，造像十万余尊。除此之外，还有麦积山、炳灵寺、天龙山、大足等几十处石窟群，造像难以胜计。这些石窟的基本特点，是依山凿崖，雕佛塑像，刀法洗练，线条流畅，姿式优美，体态生动，具有高度的艺术性和观赏性。许多石窟的内容都像一部连续剧，形象地记述了中国的悠久历史，生动地描绘了民族的灿烂文化。就是这些石窟，不断引来无数的文人学士，探求洞窟的艺术，追朔世界的奥秘。

帝王陵墓更是罕见的一大奇观。从黄帝造陵以来，秦始皇陵、汉武帝陵、唐太宗（627-659在位）陵、宋太祖陵、以及明朝的十三陵、清朝的东、西陵等，都耗费了巨大的人力和财力。其中被发掘的陵墓中，秦始皇兵马俑规模最大。据载，自他即位不久就开始建陵，长达三十七年，耗费劳工七十余万。墓中建有宫殿，设有百官位次，上有日月星辰，下有山川地理。从墓坑中可以看到，军阵浩荡，武士雄伟，展示着秦始皇率领千军万马，外抗匈奴，内平六国，统一中国的宏伟胆识，参观之后，令人叹为观止。位于北京的十三陵，是为明朝十三个皇帝建造的陵墓。其中定陵已被发掘，这里埋葬的是明朝第十四位皇帝朱翊钧（1573-1620在位）和他的两个皇后。宫内有二十六只陪葬箱子，内装珠宝玉器三千余件。地宫规模浩大，内部修饰豪华。如果你想知道地宫之迷，可到定陵地下宫殿一游，看一看皇帝生前的荣华富贵，死后的奢侈场景。

漫游神州 饱览千古胜迹

中国的文物古迹，遍及青山绿野，最有代表性的当首推宫阙殿堂。宫殿是中国建筑艺术中最辉煌的部分，在历史上，帝王登基后，都要大建宫室。秦始皇建阿房宫，连绵三百里，至秦亡犹未建成，项羽入关，焚于战火，据载大火三月不灭。唐代大明宫，据现存的含元殿和麟德殿基础遗址测算，其气魄不次于北京故宫的太和殿。现存唐九成宫图所描绘的唐代宫室，仿佛神仙楼阁。汉代的长乐宫、未央宫、长信宫等都是中国历史上著名的宫殿建筑群，因兵燹毁于一旦，已不复存在。现存最完整，最壮丽的古典建筑，尚有北京故宫、沈阳故宫、承德离宫、布达拉宫等，其特点是气势雄伟，豪华壮观，楼阁殿堂，金碧辉煌。虽经多次维修仍保持了原来布局。

园林建筑亦属文物古迹。园林可分皇家园林和官邸园林，皇家园林规模宏大，气势超群，多以真山真水为背景，层层叠建。如北京的北海公园、颐和园、圆明园、承德的避暑山庄等，山青水碧，波光塔影，绿树丛荫，殿堂隐现。而官邸园林则结构精巧，造型绝妙，假山流水都是人工建造。如苏州、杭州、无锡、扬州等地，园林繁多，造型各异。在建筑上采取了或以林掩其幽，或以山壮其势，或以水见其秀，或以石显其姿的造园手法，把景物表现得淋漓尽致，达到了建筑艺术的高峰。

佛教圣地在中国的建筑史上，占很重要的地位。它以造型独特，古朴浑厚的建筑形式，表现了中华民族的磅礴气势。最有代表性的是五台山、普陀山、九华山、峨眉山四大佛教圣地。五台山现存寺庙四十七座，台内的显通寺、镇海寺、南山寺、龙泉寺，虽说气势浩大，但屡经修葺，已不复旧貌。而台外的南禅寺、佛光寺，因避于战火，均保持了唐代的建筑原型，是中国珍贵的古建筑群之一。普陀山寺庙最多，古有"无棚不寺，无人不僧"之说，其中规模最大的普济、法雨、慧济三大寺院，建筑古朴，香火旺盛。九华山寺庙的建筑规模更大，鼎盛时期多达三百余座，僧众四千余人，享有"佛国仙城"之号。至今化城寺、祇园寺等，香火缭绕，经声不断，善男信女，络绎不绝。峨眉山初为道教，后改佛教，共建大小寺庙近百座。其中万年寺、报国寺规模最大，建筑宏伟，气势轩昂，各殿佛像，金灿夺目。除此之外，白马寺、寒山寺、少林寺、悬空寺等，还有若干道场，都是古代建筑的精华。

寺庙庵观遍布神州大地。以东岳泰山为首的西岳化山、南岳衡山、北岳恒山、中岳嵩山的文物古迹最为丰富多彩，自然景观，极为秀丽。泰山碧霞祠建筑规模宏大，祠分内外两院，碧霞元君端坐大殿正中。玉皇庙建于泰山极顶之上，祀玉皇大帝。古朴雄健，气势非凡，国内罕见。华山镇岳宫，建于玉女峰与莲花峰之间，正宫内供奉玉皇大帝。松林葱郁，清幽异常，是极好的修道圣地。衡山建有南台寺、福严寺等，最险要的是祝融殿，上攀苍穹，下临深壑，百里之外，隐约可见。恒山建有悬空寺、净土寺等十多处庙宇，值得细述的是悬空寺，该寺建于恒山金龙口的崖壁上，凿洞穴，插悬梁为基，上建殿堂楼阁四十余间，佛像八十余尊。两座大殿，南北对峙，中隔断崖，飞架栈道相通。高低错落，参差有致，饶有诗情画意。嵩山建有嵩岳寺，少林寺等十三处古建筑群，红墙黄瓦，雄伟气魄，嵩岳塔矗立于此。以上这些寺庙庵观，有的依山叠建，有的绝壁凌空，有的古松掩映，有的座落顶峰，别具风韵。

漫游神州　俯瞰无限风光

中国风光之所以引人入胜，是因为有长年不衰的自然景观，奇峰峻岭就是其中主要的组成部分。举世闻名的黄山，万壑千峰，云雾缭绕，经常出现大面积的云海。有时波涛翻滚，有时霞光万道，当奇松、怪石、云海融为一体时，景色更是无比奇伟。此刻，你会领略到天上人间的美好景象。烟云万状的武陵源，是一处极为罕见的自然景区，其中张家界、天子山、黄氏寨的风景最美。在大约八百平方公里的境内，密集着二千余座奇峰，状如石笋，拔地而起。山间万木葱茏，景色千姿百态，珍禽异兽，不时的出没在花草之中，这里是一块净化了的绿色宝地。群峰壁立的石林，是一块天然的自然景观，面积达四十余万亩。这里有著名的大石林、小石林、狮子山、紫云洞、石林湖、剑峰池等数十个景区。奇峰危石，直刺青天，远望犹如一片莽莽森林。循阶而行，曲径通幽，峰回路转，别有洞天。

江河湖海是大自然的千古杰作，自古文人就把它描绘得如诗似画，情真意惬。气势浩荡的长江水，由西向东，一泻千里。最壮观的景区是瞿塘峡、巫峡、西陵峡，两岸峭壁高耸、峡中急流汹涌，奔腾出峡的浪花，令人惊心动魄。黄河是中华民族的象征，纵观长河百折千曲，细看两岸无比粗犷。尤其那威震山谷的壶口瀑布，恰似中华民族的英雄气概。山青水秀的漓江风光，是自然景观的又一代表。这里清水幽幽，翠竹丛丛，两岸青峰叠翠，江水绕山而行。当你乘舟飘然而过的时候，人动景异，目不暇接。流光溢彩的九寨沟，浓艳神秘，周围雪峰终年不化，沟谷密布原始森林。大小湖泊百余处，形成了千奇百怪的瀑布群。这里的山水没有受到任何破坏和污染，当你身临其境，赏心悦目的时候，它会陶冶你的情操，荡涤你的心灵。

林原漠岛是中国风光的另一个侧面，从森林到平原，从沙漠到海岛，都有各自的自然风貌。江南的翠竹、长白山的白桦、新疆的胡杨，以及大兴安岭的原始森林等，葱郁青翠，茫茫苍苍，层林尽染，如火如丹，都像一幅壮观的自然画卷。辽西、华北、齐鲁、川西四大平原，渠道纵横，田肥苗壮，绿浪滚滚，辽阔茂密，又是一片迷人景象。沙漠是中国大西北独有的风采，最大的要算塔克拉玛干大沙漠了。它面积之大，漠峰之高，沙丘林立，势如锋刀。狂风骤起，黄沙蔽天，极为壮观。中国的海岛无数可计，最美丽，最繁荣的是舟山群岛。它犹如颗颗翠玉，镶嵌在碧波之中，灿烂多姿，光采四耀。神州大地，盎然生机，那"满岛绿树满岛楼，半月遥空窗外明"的神话般的世界，更令人沉思、遐想。

《漫游神州》是一本文图并茂的画册，精彩的图片和得体的文字融为一体，较全面地概括了中国的风物人情。本书既有较强的知识性和可读性，也有一定的艺术性和观赏性。一册在手，即可助你遨游神州，又可帮你丰富知识，从中了解中国的人文历史与自然风貌。

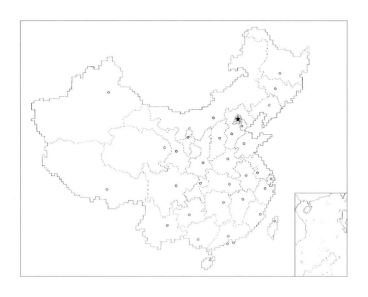

Beijing, capital of the People's Republic of China, is a cultural city with a long history. It boasts magnificent classical buildings and other cultural relics. The Forbidden City, the Temple of Heaven, Beihai Park, and the Ming Tombs symbolize essence of the architectural art of ancient China.

北京市，是中华人民共和国的首都，是一座历史悠久的文化古城。这里有宏伟的古典建筑，有众多的名胜古迹。故宫、天坛、颐和园，北海、长城、十三陵，都是最大最完整的古建筑群。气势雄伟，豪华壮丽，是中国古代建筑艺术的精华。

Watchtowers are located on all the four corners of the Forbidden City in the same design. Each is composed of nine beams, 18 pillars, three layers of eaves and 72 ridges.

角楼位于紫禁城的四角，四座角楼方向各异，造型相同，分别由九梁、十八柱、三重檐、七十二脊构成。角楼建于城墙之上，红柱黄瓦，分外俏丽。

The Palace Museum, also known as the Forbidden City, is located in the center of Beijing. It was first constructed in the Yuan Dynasty (1271-1368), and was then reconstructed in 1406 and finished in 1420. It was expanded in the Qing Dynasty (1644-1911). Some 24 emperors of the Ming (1368-1644) and Qing dynasties between 1420 and 1924 lived here. It covers an area of 720,000 square meters and has over 9,000 rooms. It is the largest and best-preserved ancient building complex in China.

故宫旧称紫禁城，位于北京市中心。始建于元代（1271-1368），明永乐四年（1406）开始重建，永乐十八年（1420）基本建成，后经清代屡加扩建，呈现规模，迄今已有五百七十多年。自公元1420年至1924年间，在这里住过明、清两代的二十四个皇帝。占地七十二万多平方米，屋子九千余间，是我国现存最大最完整的古建筑群。

The Temple of Heaven was constructed in 1420, as the place where the emperors of the Ming and Qing dynasties (1368-1911) prayed for good harvests in spring and for rain in summer and worshiped Heaven in winter.

天坛是一座古代建筑群，始建于明永乐十八年（1420）。是明清两代封建帝王孟春祈谷、夏季祈雨、冬至祀天的地方。

Beihai Park was constructed during the Five Dynasties (907-960). It is known for its historical relics, unique artistic garden, and beautiful landscape.

　　北海是我国园林建筑的瑰宝、由辽、金、元、明、清五个朝代、逐渐修造而成。它以丰富多彩的文物古迹、风格独特的造林艺术、幽美秀丽的湖光山色而驰名中外。

The Fragrant Hills is a popular leisure resort for the people of Beijing. Autumn is the best season to visit this wooded area, when the red leaves and green pine trees make the hills resplendent.

香山是北京的一大景区，山势陡峭，草木繁茂，环境幽雅，景色秀丽。尤其到了霜秋季节，红叶缤纷、层林尽染，与翠绿松柏相衬，显得格外清新醒目。

◀ The Summer Palace is the only largest and best-preserved imperial garden in China. It was originally a retreat and pleasure ground for rulers. In 1750, it was renovated and named the Pure Wave Garden. After the allied forces of Britain and France destroyed the garden in 1860, the Empress Dowager Cixi reconstructed it in 1888, using the navy budget and renamed it the Summer Palace.

颐和园是我国现存的一处规模最大和最完整的皇家园林。原为帝王的行宫和花园，清乾隆十五年（1750）改建为清漪园。1860年被英法联军所毁，光绪十四年(1888)慈禧挪用海军经费重建，改称颐和园。

The Temple of Azure Clouds was first built in 1516 by the eunuch Yu Jing. In 1748, the Hall of Arhats and the Diamond Throne Pagoda were constructed. The hall, oriented in an east-west direction in front of a mountain, is surrounded by pine and cypress trees.

碧云寺原称碧云庵。明正德十一年(1516)太监于经在庵后得建寺院，始称今名。清乾隆十三年(1748)，增建罗汉堂和金刚宝塔。寺庙座东向西、依山叠建、松柏参天、浓荫蔽日，金刚宝塔立于其中。

The Ruins of Yuanmingyuan (Old Summer Palace) used to be a large imperial garden of the Qing Dynasty (1644-1911). It was first constructed in 1709 and completed in 1744, with over 140 towers, terraces, halls, and pavilions. In 1860, the allied forces of Britain and France looted it and burned it to the ground. Only the ruins of stone sculptures of the Garden of Everlasting Spring remain.

　　圆明园遗址。圆明园原是清代的一座大型皇家御苑，始建于康熙四十八年(1709)，乾隆九年(1744)基本建成。园内建有楼台殿阁、亭榭轩馆一百四十余处。咸丰十年(1860)，英法联军劫掠园中珍宝，并纵火焚毁，现今仅存长春园西洋楼的部分石雕残迹。

The Ming Tombs are the last resting-places of 13 emperors of the Ming Dynasty. The tomb area faces south, flanked by Dragon Hill and Tiger Hill lining at the two sides, forming a natural gate. The tombs were constructed over a period of 230 years. Only the tomb of Emperor Wanli (reigned from 1573 to 1620) has been excavated so far, and visitors can view his "underground palace."

十三陵是明代十三个皇帝的陵墓。陵区座北向南、群峰耸立、南面的龙山与虎山分列左右，犹如天然门户。明朝为了修建这十三个皇帝的陵墓，共花费了二百三十余年的时间。其中埋葬万历(公元1573-1620在位)皇帝的定陵已被发掘，从中可以领略森然肃穆的地宫格局。

Jiayuguan Pass, located in the southwest corner of Jiayuguan City of Gansu Province, is the western end of the Great Wall as well as the largest pass of the Great Wall built in the Ming Dynasty (1368-1644). The watchtowers and beacon towers are in pairs, forming a closely guarded and complete defense system.

嘉峪关位于甘肃省嘉峪关市西南隅，是明长城由东而西的终止点。也是明长城规模最大的关城、东西建立体城楼、角楼、敌楼相互对应、整个城楼贯通、构成一个壁垒森严的完整防御体系。

The Great Wall at Badaling is located in Yanqing County in the suburbs of Beijing. It was a strategic pass because of its high hills and deep valleys. In the early 16th century, the Ming Dynasty reconstructed this section on the ruins of the Great Wall built by former dynasties.

八达岭长城位于北京市延庆县境内，是长城的一个隘口。这里山高谷深，形式险要，历来是兵家必争之地。十六世纪初，明王朝为防御外来侵略，在前朝长城遗址上重新修筑新的长城，使八达岭长城和关城墙高城固，气势磅礴，如同一把铁锁扼住了北京要冲。

Shanhaiguan Pass, located northeast of Qinhuangdao, Hebei Province, serves as the eastern starting point of the 5,000-kilometer Great Wall. It faces the Bohai Sea in the east and is linked up with mountains in the west, hence its name (shan means "mountain," while hai means "sea"). It is a narrow pass that once commanded control of passage between the north China Plain and the Northeast. The terrace is 12 meters high and the city tower is 13.7 meters high. Xiao Xian, a Ming Dynasty official, wrote the inscription for the signboard on the city gate: "No.1 Pass under Heaven".

山海关位于河北省秦皇岛东北向、是万里长城的始发点。东临渤海、西接群峰、因在山与海之间而得名。此关是东北与华北之间的咽喉要冲、历史上为兵家必争之地。城台高十二米、城楼高十三米七。城门匾额"天下第一关"五个大字、出自明朝进士萧显之手。

The Great Wall at Jiaoshan Hill is the highest point guarding the Shanhaiguan Pass. It is 519 meters above sea level, and very precipitous. Tourists have to climb up a narrow ladder to reach a watchtower built on a rock.

角山长城是守卫山海关的制高点、在关城北二公里处、海拔五百一十九米、山势陡峭、顺山而下的城墙台阶有的高达九十公分。敌楼耸立于角山一块嵯峨巨石之上、游人只能攀扶窄梯而上。

The Great Wall at Simatai stretches for several thousand meters on the mountain ridges east of the Simatai Reservoir. Viewing Beijing Tower is the highest point at Simatai. It is said that one can see the lights of Beijing from here on an autumn night.

司马台长城长约数千米、建于司马台水库以东的山脊之上。长城随陡峭的山势翻上跃下、甚为险峻。望京楼是司马台的最高点、据说、在秋高气爽的夜晚、站在敌楼处、可以望见北京的灯光。

The Great Wall at Jinshanling is located to the west of Simatai Reservoir. It has watchtowers every 100 meters. In some places where the topography is complicated, the distance between two watchtowers is only 50 meters. The watchtowers are designed differently and provide valuable data for research on the architecture of the Great Wall.

金山岭长城位于司马台水库以西。它的建筑特点是敌楼密集、一般均在百米左右一座、在地形复杂处、敌楼的间距仅五十米左右。建筑形式各种各样、是研究长城建筑的集中代表。

The Great Wall at Mutianyu is located in Huairou County, 70 kilometers from Beijing city proper. It was first constructed in 1404. Most of the gate towers are built on the ridges of precipitous cliffs.

慕田峪长城位于北京怀柔县境内、距北京城区七十公里。公元1404年正式建城立关、这里的城楼多建于山体外侧的陡峭岩边之上、城墙前后两边均有垛口。

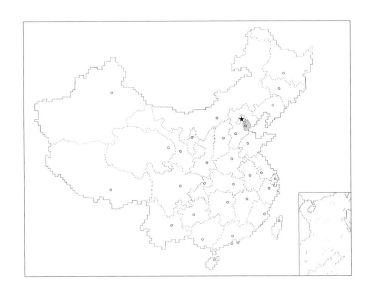

Tianjin is located in the northeastern part of the North China Plain, with the Bohai Sea to the east and Beijing Municipality to the west. The city is famous for its drum tower, Confucius Temple, Hanging Stone and Pangu Temple. Aquatic Park, with its pavilions, towers, green streams and beautiful flowers, is ideal for relaxing.

天津市位于华北平原的东北部，东临渤海湾，西接北京市。市区内有鼓楼、文庙、悬空石、盘谷寺，以及著名的水上公园。亭台楼阁，溪水碧绿，千姿百态，交相辉映，构成了一幅幽静雅致的美景。

The Confucius Temple is located in the east gate of the old city area of Tianjin. It is composed of the Lingxing Gate, Dacheng Gate, Dacheng Hall and Chongsheng Memorial Hall. The Dacheng Hall was first constructed in 1436, serving as the largest site of cultural relics in Tianjin.

文庙位于天津旧城东门，此庙实为孔庙，因与武庙相对，故称文庙。文庙是一座完整的古典建筑群，有棂星门、大成门、大成殿崇圣祠等。其中大成殿始建于明正统元年(1436)，建筑精巧，气势非凡，是天津最大的一处文物古迹。

The Aquatic Park in Tianjin, built on 13 islets in the Haihe Gulf, is a tranquil place. Arched bridges link the islets together. The water surface covers two-fifths of the total area of the park, which has the ambience of southern China. The classical buildings harmonize with the natural scenery.

天津水上公园是一个非常幽静的地方，建筑在海河湾的十三个小岛之上，岛与岛由曲桥相连。水面占全园面积的五分之二，有江南水乡的意韵。自然景色与古代建筑融为一体，令人赏心悦目。

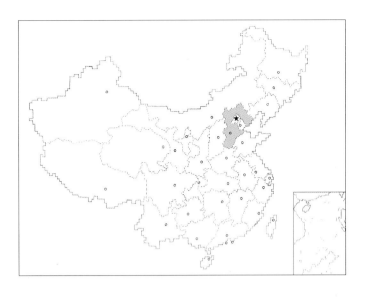

Hebei Province is located to the north of the lower reaches of the Yellow River. Famous places of cultural interest include the Eastern and Western tombs of the Qing Dynasty, Pilu Temple, Zhaozhou Bridge, Cangyan Hill, Beidaihe Summer Resort and Handan City. The magnificent Ligong Palace and the outer eight temples grace Chengde.

　河北省位于黄河下游以北。这里著名的文物古迹有清东陵、清西陵、毗卢寺、赵州桥、苍岩山、北戴河，以及赵国古都邯郸市。都是历史悠久，景色宜人的旅游胜地。特别是承德离宫，巍峨壮观，气势非凡，具有民族特色的外八庙，形成了规模宏大的宗教文化景区。

Jinshan Temple is located in the Imperial Summer Resort of Chengde, Hebei Province. Emperor Kangxi (reigned from 1662 to 1722) of the Qing Dynasty, impressed with the scenery in southern China, ordered that a replica of the scenery of Jinshan in Jiangsu Province be built in Chengde.

　金山寺位于河北省承德市避暑山庄内。此建筑是清朝皇帝康熙(公元1662-1722 在位)南巡时，看到江苏镇江金山景物，颇为欣赏，于是令下属将此景遗置山庄内澄湖东侧。建筑设计，玲珑精巧，前高后低，主次有别，匠心独运。

Water Pavilions are located in the north of the East Palace of the Chengde Imperial Summer Resort, linking the palace area with Chenghu Area. There are three pavilions on the water, forming a picturesque scene, together with the surrounding environment.

水心榭位于东宫之北，是宫殿区与澄湖区的重要通道。上列亭榭三座，跨水为桥，两旁空间辽阔，碧波荡漾，眺望四方，如诗似画，引人入胜。

Puning Temple, located in the north of the Chengde Imperial Summer Resort, is one of the eight outer temples. It is also known as Giant Buddha Temple for there is a huge wooden Buddha in it. It was first built in 1755, with many pagodas, terraces and pavilions, integrating the architectural characteristics of Han and Tibetan temples.

普宁寺位于避暑山庄北，属外八庙之一。因寺内有巨大木雕佛像，又称大佛寺。建于乾隆二十年（1755），该寺规模宏大，气势非凡，塔台罗列，崇阁入云，表现了汉藏寺庙的建筑特点。

The Eastern Tombs of the Qing Dynasty (1644-1911), located in Malanyu, Zunhua County, Hebei Province, are tombs of members of the imperial family of the Qing Dynasty. There are five emperors buried here, including Emperor Shunzhi in the Xiaoling Tomb, Emperor Kangxi in the Jingling Tomb, Emperor Qianlong in the Yuling Tomb, Emperor Xianfeng in the Dingling Tomb and Emperor Tongzhi in the Huiling Tomb. There are also four empresses' tombs, five concubines' tombs, and one princess's tomb.

清东陵位于河北省遵化县马兰峪，是清朝皇室的陵墓群。陵有帝陵五座，即：孝陵顺治、景陵康熙、裕陵乾隆、定陵咸丰、慧陵同治。后陵四座，妃陵五座，公主陵一座。以孝陵为中心，构成一个井然有序的封建王族体系。

The Western Tombs of the Qing Dynasty (1644-1911) are located at the foot of Yongning Mountain in Yixian County, Hebei Province. Emperor Qianlong ordered that he and his sons should not be buried together. There are four emperors' tombs in the Western Tombs, including the Tailing Tomb of Emperor Yongzheng, the Changling Tomb of Emperor Jiaqing, the Muling Tomb of Emperor Daoguang and Chongling Tomb of Emperor Guangxu. In addition, there are three empresses' tombs, three concubines' tombs, and four princes' and princesses' tombs. The tombs cover a large area with countless pine and cypress trees around them.

清西陵位于河北省易县永宁山下。当年乾隆帝有诏定，父子不葬一地之制，相间在东西陵分葬。西陵有帝陵四座，即：泰陵雍正、昌陵嘉庆、慕陵道光、崇陵光绪。后陵三座，妃陵三座，王公、公主四座。陵区内林木一望无际。

Shanxi Province, located in the west of the Central North Plain and on the middle reaches of the Yellow River, abounds in historical relics, such as the Memorial Temple of Jin, Shuanlin Temple, Yongle Palace, Hukou Waterfall, Yungang Grottoes (one of the three biggest grotto complexes in China), Mount Wutai (one of the four Buddhist shrines in China), and Mount Hengshan (one of the five famous mountains in China).

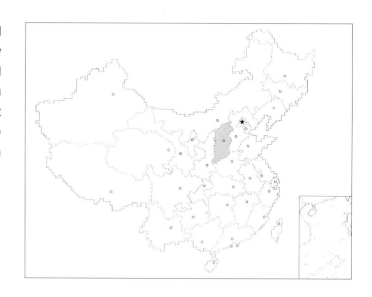

山西省位于华北平原以西、黄河中游地区，这里有众多的文物古迹。晋祠、双林寺、永乐宫、壶口瀑布，以及列入中国三大石窟之一的云冈窟，中国佛教四大名山之一的五台山、中国五岳之一的北岳恒山，均在于此。以上这些文物古迹，历经风雨，依然风采如故。

Jin Memorial Temple is located 25 kilometers southwest of Taiyuan, capital of Shanxi Province. It was first built in 1023. The Goddess Hall is the main building of the temple with a fishpond in front and a precipitous hill behind. There are 43 colored clay sculptures dating back to the Song Dynasty (960-1279), with the statue of the goddess as the main one. All the statues have vivid expressions and postures.

晋祠位于山西省太原市西南二十五公里处，始建于北宋年间(1023)。圣母殿是晋祠的主体建筑，前临鱼沼，后拥危峰，整体建筑十分自然。殿内有宋代彩塑四十三尊，主像为圣母，塑像表现得口有情、眼有神、姿态生动、神情各异，是我国宋塑中的精品。

Mount Wutai, located in Wutai County, Shanxi Province, is one of the four famous Buddhist shrines in China. The hills are undulating, the temples are magnificent and house many cultural relics. It looks like a holy land of Buddhism adorned with pine and cypress trees.

　　五台山是中国佛教四大名山之一，位于山西省五台县境内。这里山峦起伏，寺庙巍峨，殿堂悠久，文物众多，苍松翠柏，参差其间，一派佛教圣地风光。

Mount Hengshan, located in Hunyuan County in Shanxi Province, is one of the five famous mountains in China. The Hanging Temple is a special wonder of Mount Hengshan. The temple was first built in the 6th century on the western cliff of Jinlongkou at the foot of the Mountain. There are 40 halls, towers and pavilions, and over 80 statues in the temple.

　　恒山是中国著名的五岳之一，位于山西省浑源县境内。悬空寺是恒山的一大奇观，建在恒山脚下的金龙口西崖的峭壁上。始建于北魏六世纪，全寺有殿宇楼阁四十间，雕像八十余尊。登楼俯视如临深渊；谷底仰视悬崖若虹。

Shuanglin Temple is located in Pingyao County, Shanxi Province. It was first constructed in 571, and was renovated in the Ming Dynasty (1368-1644). Most of the buildings and statues remained are left from the Ming Dynasty. There are many colored clay statues in the temple, all with different postures, making the temple an art museum.

双林寺位于山西省平遥县。该寺建于北齐武平二年(571)，明代曾多次重建。现存建筑和塑像大多是明代遗物。双林寺彩塑林立，造型各异，俨然是一座精美的艺术馆。

The Yungang Grottoes are located on Wuzhou Mountain, Datong City, Shanxi Province. The carvings of the grottoes, one of largest groups in China, started in the year 453. At present, 53 grottoes remain, with 51,000 exquisitely designed statues.

云冈石窟位于山西省大同市武周山上。始凿于北魏兴安二年(453)，现存主要洞窟五十三个，造像五万一千余尊，是我国最大的石窟之一。雕工精细、刚健浑厚，是我国闻名的艺术宝库。

Hukou Waterfall on the Yellow River is located in Jixian County, Shanxi Province. The roaring of the river can be heard miles away.

黄河壶口瀑布位于山西省吉县境内。此地两岸夹水、河水奔流、倒悬倾注 。形如巨壶沸腾、惊涛怒吼、声震数里、不绝于耳。

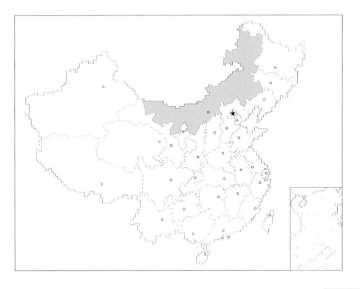

The Inner Mongolia Autonomous Region, located in northern China, borders Russia and Mongolia. The Hulun Bur Grassland, Erhkuna River, Daji Lake, Moyu Lake and Genghis Khan Mausoleum are all musts for tourists. The Ewenki ethnic group lives in the primitive forests of the Greater Hinggan Mountains in the region.

内蒙古自治区位于中国的北部边疆，与俄罗斯和蒙古国接壤。这里有呼伦贝尔草原、额尔古纳河、以及达赉湖、墨玉湖、武当召、成吉思汗陵等，水草茂密，牛羊成群，构成一幅壮丽画卷。尤其在大兴安岭在原始森林中，还有过着原始生活的鄂温克族，更是值得到此一游。

The Inner Mongolian Grassland is one of the five main herding areas in China. Forests adorn the west slopes of the Great Hinggan Mountains. The endless wild grass, colorful flowers and slow-running brooks are ideal for raising cows and sheep.

内蒙古草原是中国五大牧区之一。从大兴安岭西坡开始，由东而西，有森林草原、草甸草原、典型草原等，不同类型的大草原展向天际。这里野草葱葱、鲜花朵朵、弯曲的河流缓慢地流向远方。大自然的恩赐不仅使这里的水草丰茂，牛羊肥壮，而且造就了蒙古族人民强健豪爽的性格。

The Erhkuna River, located on the upper reaches of the Heilongjiang River, is a boundary river between China and Russia, with a length of 1,608 kilometers. It has a number of tributaries, including the Hailaer and Genhe rivers. Every spring, the fish and shrimp in these unpolluted rivers attract thousands of fishermen.

额尔古纳河是黑龙江的上游，中俄界河，全长一千六百零八公里。有海拉尔河、根河等数条支流注入，水量大，水质好，没有污染。每当春雷鸣响，鱼成队，虾成群，引来无数垂钓爱好者，别有一番兴致。

Hulun Lake, also known as Dalai Lake, is the fifth largest lake in China, with a surface area of 2,339 square kilometers. The blue sky, green river, white clouds and broad fields seem to be in perfect harmony.

呼伦湖又称达赉湖, 属于中国第五大湖。水面二千三百三十九平方公里、融蓝天、碧水、白云、绿野为一体, 令人赞叹不已。湖面百鸟戏飞, 水中鱼虾翻挺, 日可观朝夕霞光, 夜可闻浪潮推涌。湖中有岛、岛上有湖, 酷似引颈高飞的仙鹤。

Moyu (Blackish Green Jade) Lake, located in the northeast of Wuliangsu Sea, is like a piece of jade on the grassland. In autumn, the sky is blue, the water green, the fields yellow and the reed catkins fragrant.

墨玉湖位于乌梁素海东北向、进入秋季, 天空湛蓝, 湖水碧绿, 苇田金黄, 芦花飘香, 墨玉湖显得更加深邃黝亮, 就像一块"金镶玉"镶嵌在绿色草原上。

Primitive forests in the Great Hinggan Mountains, in Inner Mongolia, cover an area of 5.4 million hectares. Some 2,000 species of wild plants grow in the Wuling area, east of the mountains.

大兴安岭原始森林，位于呼伦贝尔盟境内、总面积达五百四十万公顷。有两千多种野生植物，生长在大兴安岭以东的五陵地带。

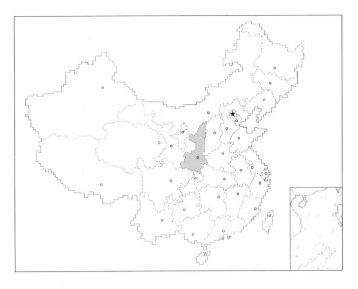

Shaanxi Province, located in the central-northern part of China and on the middle reaches of the Yellow River, is famous for its Emperor Qin Shi Huang Mausoleum, Yellow Emperor Mausoleum, Maoling Tomb, Qianling Tomb, Xi'an ancient city, Banpo Neolithic ruins, Greater Wild Goose Pagoda, Lesser Wild Goose Pagoda, Famen Temple and Huaqing Pool. Mount Huashan, one of the five famous mountains in China and a tourist destination, is also located here.

陕西省位于中国的中北部，黄河流域的中游。举世闻名的秦始皇陵、黄帝陵、茂陵、乾陵、西安古城、半坡遗址、大雁塔、小雁塔、法门寺、华清池等，都闪烁着历史的光辉。著名的中国五岳之一华山，亦在于此，险峰苍松，奇拔峻秀，是中外游人的好去处。

The Great Wild Goose Pagoda is located in the Ci'en Temple, four kilometers south of Xi'an, capital of Shaanxi Province. It gets its name from a legend about a mysterious goose, thought to have been a deity, which fell out of the sky on this spot. In 652 of the Tang Dynasty, Xuanzang, the abbot, had the temple constructed in an attempt to protect the Buddhist scriptures which he had brought from India.

大雁塔在陕西省西安市南四公里的慈恩寺内。据《慈恩寺三藏法师传》载"摩揭陀国有一僧寺，一日有群鸿飞过，忽一雁离群落羽，摔死地上，僧人惊异，认为雁即菩萨，众议埋雁建塔，而故名，唐永徽三年(652)，慈恩寺主持僧玄奘为保护由印度带回的经籍，由唐高宗资助而建。

The Museum of Emperor Qin Shi Huang's Terracotta Army is located in the eastern part of the emperor's mausoleum. Some of the terracotta warriors hold bows, and some hold swords or knives. The horses and warriors all face east.

秦始皇陵兵马俑博物馆位于秦始皇陵东侧。是一个以掏塑为阵容的兵马俑葬坑，有的手执弓箭，有的手执矛戟等兵器，或负弩前驱、或御车策马、万余卫士、面向东方，排列在葬坑之中。

Huo Qubing's Tomb is located 500 meters east of the Maoling Tomb in Xingping County, Shaanxi Province. Huo Qubing was a famous Western Han (206BC-A.D.24) general who conducted six campaigns against the western tribes, conquering the Hexi Corridor and Xinjiang. He died at the age of 24 in 117 BC. A stele was erected in front of his tomb, with an inscription by Emperor Wudi of the Western Han Dynasty.

霍去病墓在兴平县茂陵东五百米处，是汉武帝刘彻(前140-87在位)陵的陪葬墓之一。霍去病十八岁随卫青出征匈奴、曾先后六次出击、打通河西走廊与西域之间的交通。元狩六年(前117)病死，年仅二十四岁。墓前陈列着大型圆雕石刻，是汉武帝为了表彰霍去病的战功而立的墓饰、石刻题材新颖、生动逼真、雕刻简练浑厚。

Huaqing (Hot Spring) Pool, located at the foot of Lishan Mountain in Lintong County, is one of the famous hot springs in Shaanxi Province. It is said that water from the hot spring cured a skin ailment suffered by Emperor Qin Shi Huang (reigned from 246 to 209 BC), China's first emperor. In 644, Tangquan Palace was built here, and it was expanded and renamed Huaqing Pool in 747. Emperor Xuanzong of the Tang Dynasty (618-907) often came here to bathe with his favorite concubine Yang Yuhuan.

华清池位于临潼县城南骊山脚下，是陕西有名的温泉之一。相传秦始皇(前246-209在位)在骊山触怒神女，被唾一脸，后即生疮，始皇求恕，神女用温泉水给他洗好。唐贞观十八年(644)在此建汤泉宫、天宝六年(747)再行扩建，更名华清池。唐玄宗每年携贵妃到此过冬，沐浴。这里有莲花汤、九龙汤、贵妃池等，园林幽静，景色宜人。

Mount Huashan, located in Huayin County, Shaanxi Province, is one of the five famous mountains in China, with the Weishui River in the north and the Qinling Mountains in the south. The highest peak is 2,154 meters high. There is only one path leading to the top hill.

华山是中国著名的五岳之一，在华阴县境内。北临渭水，南依秦岭，主峰海拔二千一百五十四米。华山有五峰环耸，犹如一朵盛开的莲花。华山奇峰矗立，绝壁险峻，如欲登山，只有一路相通，而且徒险难攀。俗话说：自古华山一条路”，并非夸大之词。

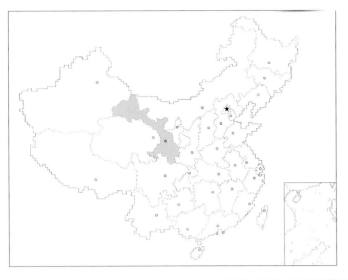

甘肃省位于黄河上游，西北与蒙古接壤。这里的古代文化遗址，有嘉峪关、鸣沙山、千佛洞、月牙泉和拉卜楞寺等。最著名的还是石窟艺术，如麦积山石窟、文殊山石窟、炳灵寺石窟、敦煌莫高窟等，艺术造诣精湛，形象丰满潇洒，富有朝气和生命力。

Gansu Province, located on the upper reaches of the Yellow River, has many famous spots, including Jiayu Pass, Singing Sands Mountain, Thousand-Buddha Cave, Crescent Moon Spring and Labrang Monastery. The most famous attraction is the grottoes on Maiji Mountain, Mountain of Lord of Wisdom, Bingling Temple, and the Dunhuang Grottoes.

Maiji Mountain Grottoes are located in Tianshui County, Gansu Province. It is said that the grottoes were first carved and the temple was first built in the Later Qin (384-417). At present, some 194 grottoes of successive dynasties remain, with 7,000 clay sculptures, and 1,300 square meters of frescoes.

麦积山石窟位于甘肃天水县境内，因此处崛起一峰，似农家积麦之状，故得此名。相传后秦时开窟造像，创建佛寺。现存历代洞窟一百九十四个、泥塑、雕塑七千余身，壁画一千三百多平方米。生活气息浓厚，令人倍感亲切。

40

The Bingling Temple Grottoes are located in Yongjing County, Gansu Province, with 183 niches, 679 stone statues of Buddha and 900 square meters of frescoes dating from the Western Qin (385-431) to the Qing Dynasty (1644-1911).

炳椻寺石窟位于甘肃省永靖县境内、自西秦到明、清、建窟龛一百八十三个、石雕佛像六百七十九尊、壁画九百平方米。窟龛凿于南北峭壁、长约两公里、上下四层、高低错落。

Mogao Grottoes in Dunhuang are located 35 kilometers to the southeast of Dunhuang County in Gansu Province. Work on the grottoes started in 366, and by the Tang Dynasty (618-907) there were over 1,000 grottoes. At present, only 492 grottoes, 45,000 square meters of frescoes and 2,400 colored clay sculptures of successive dynasties are preserved.

敦煌莫高窟位于甘肃省敦煌县城东南三十五公里处。莫高窟始建于前秦建元二年(336)，至唐代武则天时。已有窟室千余。现尚保存历代壁画和塑像的洞窟四百九十二个，壁画四万五千多平方米，彩塑二千四百余尊。是一座由建筑、绘画、雕塑组成的综合艺术馆。

Labrang Monastery, located in the west of Xiahe County, Gansu Province, was constructed in 1709, serving as one of the six-largest monasteries of the Gelug Sect of Lamaism in China. The Shouxi Hall has six floors and houses a huge bronze Buddha.

拉卜楞寺在甘肃省夏河县城西，始建于清康熙四十八年(1709)，是我国喇嘛教格鲁派六大寺院之一。其中首禧殿高六层，内供铜像一尊，信徒络绎不绝。

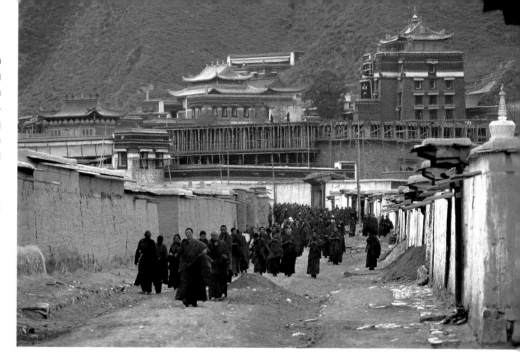

The Yellow River is the second-longest river in China. It originates in Qinghai Province, and runs past high mountains in Qinghai, Sichuan, and Gansu provinces; grasslands and deserts in the Ningxia and Inner Mongolia autonomous regions; plateaus and valleys in Shaanxi and Shanxi provinces, the grasslands of Henan and Shandong provinces and enters the Bohai Sea, with a total length of 5,464 kilometers. The Yellow River Valley was the cradle of the ancient Chinese civilization.

黄河是中国的第二条大河流。发源于青海省巴颜喀拉山北麓，穿过青海、四川、甘肃三省的崇山峻岭；流过宁夏、内蒙的平原大漠；转而陕西、山西的高原深谷；东折河南、山东的大平原注入渤海，全长五千四百六十四公里。黄河流域是中华民族古代文明的摇篮。

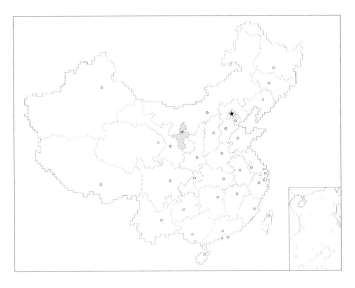

The Ningxia Hui Autonomous Region is located on the middle reaches of the Yellow River at the foot of the Helan Mountains. Yinchuan City is famous for many places of historical interest, including eight tombs of kings of the Western Xia Kingdom, the Great Wall of the Qin Dynasty, Liupan Mountain Grottoes, and the Xumi Mountain Grottoes, Shikong Temple and Zhongweigao Grottoes, as well as 108 pagodas.

宁夏回族自治区位于黄河上游，在银川市西三十公里处的贺兰山下，有西夏历代帝王陵墓八座和七十余座陪葬墓。秦长城、六盘山、须弥山石窟、石空寺石窟、中卫高石窟、一百零八塔等，都是中国的重要文化遗迹。

The tombs of kings of Western Xia are located west of Yinchuan, capital of the Ningxia Hui Autonomous Region. The area of the eight mausoleums measures 10 kilometers from south to north, and four kilometers from east to west.

西夏王陵位于宁夏银川市西，约三十公里处的贺兰山东麓，是西夏历代帝王陵墓的所在地。陵区范围南北十公里，东西四公里，随地形错落着八座西夏帝王的陵园和十余座陪葬墓。

The Xumi Mountain Grottoes are located east of Mount Xumi, 60 kilometers from the seat of Guyuan County, in the Ningxia Hui Autonomous Region. The grottoes were the dwelling places of Buddhist monks. The work of carving started in the Northern Wei (386-534). Only 20 grottoes remain so far, lengthening two kilometers.

须弥山石窟位于固原县城西北六十公里处的须弥山东麓。这里峰峦叠嶂、岩石嶙峋，是凿仙窟以居禅的好地方。从北朝(386-534)北魏起，历代都在此营造窟室，现存较完整的有二十余窟，长约二公里。

This statue of Sakyamuni is in the fifth Xumi Mountain Grotto. It is 20 meters high. The statues on Mount Xumi share the common characteristics of full and round faces, and calm expressions.

释迦牟尼像是须弥山五号窟的主佛像，高二十多米。须尔山造像的特点是、面型丰满、表情安详，是研究我国石窟艺术的珍贵资料。

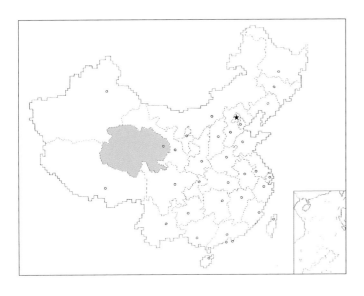

Qinghai Province is located in the northeast of the Qinghai-Tibet Plateau. The Ta'er Monastery in Huangzhong County was constructed in 1560, as one of the six temples of the Gelugs Sect of Tibetan Buddhism. Qutan Temple, Wutun Temple, Qinghai Lake and Temple of Princess Wencheng are all important tourist destinations.

青海省位于青藏高原的东北部。在湟中县境内有著名的塔尔寺，始建于明嘉靖三十九年(1560)，是中国喇嘛教格鲁派六大寺院之一。另外，瞿昙寺、五屯寺、青海湖，以及文成公主庙等，均属中外文化交流的重要组成部分。

Ta'er Monastery, located to the southwest of Lusha'er Town, Huangzhong County, Qinghai Province, was first constructed in 1560. It is one of the six-largest monasteries of Gelug Sect of Tibetan Buddhism in China. The monastery, composed of 11 buildings including Big Golden Tile Palace, Small Golden Tile Palace, Small Flower Temple and Big Scripture Hall, is the center of Buddhist activities in northwest China.

塔尔寺位于湟中县鲁沙尔镇西南隅。始建于明嘉靖三十九年(1560)，是我国喇嘛教格鲁派六大寺院之一。有小金瓦、大金瓦、小花寺、大经堂等十一处建筑，是我国西北地区佛教活动的中心。

Qinghai Lake is located between Mount Datong and Mount Riyue in the northeast of Qinghai Province. It is the largest inland saltwater lake in China. Seven rivers, including the Ganzi and Shaliu, flow into the lake. Every spring, thousands of birds make temporary homes on the five islands of the lake.

青海湖古称西湖，位于青海省东北大通山、日月山间。是我国最大的内陆咸水湖，主要水源有甘子河、沙柳河等七条主要河流汇集湖中，有五个岛屿。每年春季有十万多只斑头雁、天鹅等鸟类来此，这里是鸟的世界。

The Xinjiang Uygur Autonomous Region, located in the far northwest of China, borders India, Pakistan, Tadzhikistan, Kirghzstan, Kazakhstan, Russia and Mongolia. The Heavenly Lake, located on the Bogda Peak in Fukang County, is a very popular tourist destination. In addition, there are Flaming Mountain, Turpan, Guozi Valley at the foot of the Tianshan Mountains and Sayram Lake.

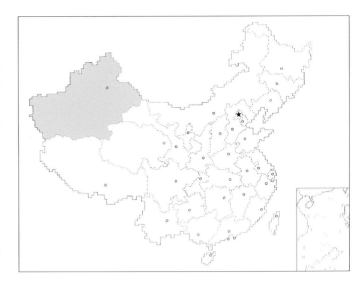

新疆维吾尔自治区地处中国西北边疆。与印度、巴基斯坦、阿富汗、塔吉克斯坦、吉尔吉斯斯坦、哈萨克斯坦、俄罗斯及蒙古国接壤。在阜康县境内的博格达峰山腰间，有一"天池"，古称"瑶池"，是著名的游览胜地。还有红砂岩构成的火焰山、吐鲁番、天山下的果子沟、以及博乐县的赛里木湖，都是新疆的主要风景区。

Turpan Mosque is one of the largest mosques in Xinjiang Uygur Autonomous Region, covering an area of one hectare. The entrance gate is huge linking with the left and right halls. Some white designs were painted on the gray brick wall, leaving an impression of solemnity and magnificence.

吐鲁番清真寺是新疆最大的寺庙之一，占地约十五亩，高大的寺门巍峨屹立，与左右配厅相接，构成了一个整体。在灰色的砖面上勾画着银白色的图案，给人以庄严、肃穆、宏伟、壮丽的感觉。

Flaming Mountain, located in the center of the Turpan Basin, is 500 meters above sea level, lengthening 100 kilometers from east to west and 10 kilometers from south to north. The red sandstone of the mountain looks like flames in the blazing sunshine.

火焰山位于吐鲁番盆地中部。东西长达一百公里，南北宽约十公里，海拔约五百米，主要为红砂岩所构成。因夏季气候干热，在强烈阳光照射下，红色砂岩熠熠发光，宛若阵阵烈火。

Guozi Valley is located in the Tianshan Mountains, in the north of Xinjiang. It is on the route of the old Silk Road, which linked China with Europe.

果子沟位于新疆北部的天山丛中。沟长二十八公里，地势险要，自古就是我国中原人民通往亚、欧的一条重要孔道，是伊宁至乌鲁木齐公路必经之地。夹岸峰峦耸峙，松桦繁茂，泉流清冷，山路曲折，更引人入胜。

Lake Tianchi (Heavenly Lake), located in the halfway up the Bogda Peak in the Tianshan Mountains, is a famous tourist spot. It is formed of glacier water, and is 1,900 meters above sea level and 90 meters deep.

天池位于天山博格达峰山腰，是著名的旅游胜地。海拔一千九百米，湖深九十米，系高山溶雪汇集而成。湖水清澈，绿如碧玉，四周雪峰环抱，云杉参天，景色十分壮丽。

Sayram Lake, located in Bole County, Xinjiang Uygur Autonomous Region, is the highest lake above sea level in China and covers an area of 457 square kilometers. There are three islands in the south of the lake. The lake, surrounded by hills on four sides, enjoys a beautiful natural scenery.

赛里木湖位于新疆西部博乐县。湖水面积四百五十七平方公里，是新疆海拔最高的高山湖。南有三岛，建有龙王庙，绿草如茵，水色清碧。四周群山环抱，雪峰倒映水中，令人心旷神怡。

The snowy peaks of Bogda Mountain are located in Fukang County, Changji Hui Autonomous Prefecture, in Xinjiang. The snow on the mountain does not melt for the whole year.

博格达山雪峰位于新疆昌吉回族自治州阜康县境内。山上积雪终年不消，世称雪海，三峰并立，高矗云霄，极为壮观。

Shandong Province is located on the lower reaches of the Yellow River between the Bohai Sea and the Yellow Sea. Famous scenic spots include the 72 springs of Jinan, Huiquan Gulf in Qingdao, the site of Dawenkou Culture in Qin'an, the Penglai Pavilion, and Confucius Temple in Qufu. Mount Taishan, the highest among the five famous mountains in China, is an ideal summer resort.

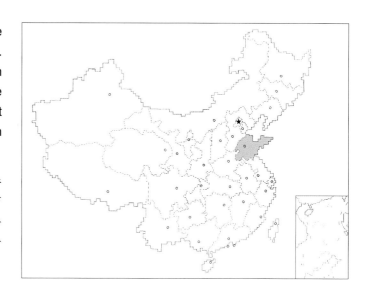

山东省位于黄河下游、东临渤海与黄海之间、北与辽东半岛相望。这里有济南市的七十二泉、青岛市的汇泉湾、秦安市的大汶口文化、蓬莱市的蓬莱阁、曲阜市的孔庙、著名的五岳之首泰山气势雄伟，峰峦峻拔，殿宇辉煌，苍松茂密。是避暑游览之胜地。

Daimiao Temple, located at the foot of Mount Taishan, Shandong Province, is the place where emperors held ceremonies to worship the God of Mount Taishan. The temple was first built in the Qin Dynasty (221-206BC) and was then expanded in the Song Dynasty (960-1279).

岱庙位于山东省泰安市泰山脚下，是封建帝王举行封禅大典祭祀泰山神的地方。创建于秦汉之际，宋代拓建至此规模。整个庙宇高大雄伟，富丽堂皇，是典型的宫殿式建筑。

51

Bixia Memorial Hall on the Jade Emperor Peak is a magnificent building constructed during Emperor Zhengzong's reign (998-1022).

　　碧霞祠位于玉皇顶庙前，是祭礼碧霞元君的庙堂。宋真宗(998-1022在位)东封泰山时所建，是岱顶的一座宏伟建筑。

Mount Taishan, located in Shandong Province is the most famous mountain in China. It is 21 kilometers from Daimiao Temple to Jade Emperor Peak, with 6,293 steps.

　　泰山是中国著名的五岳之首，位于泰安市北。从岱庙至玉皇顶，约行二十一公里，其中蹬道就达六千二百九十三级，逐级而上直达南天门。

Viewing-the-Sunrise Peak, located to the east of the Jade Emperor Peak, serves as a place to view the sunrise. Arching North Rock in the northern part of the peak is the best spot for this.

　　日观峰位于玉皇顶东，是岱顶的观日出的地方。峰北侧有一巨石，悬空探出，长约二丈，名拱北石，也称探海石。在这里可看四大奇观的"旭日东升"。

Confucius Temple, located in Qufu City, Shandong Province, has 460 halls and rooms. Measuring one kilometer from south to north, it is the largest temple in China with 460 halls and rooms.

孔庙在曲阜市内、南接旧城垣、东与孔府毗邻、是历代祭祀孔子的地方。全庙共有殿堂阁室四百六十间、南北长一公里、苍松古柏、森然罗列、是我国现存最大的庙宇。

Daming Lake, located in the north of Jinan, capital of Shandong Province, is famous for its many springs, including the Pearl Spring, Hibiscus Spring and Imperial Palace Pond, covering an area of 46.5 hectares. There are many sightseeing towers, terraces, pavilions and corridors along the lake.

大明湖位于山东济南市城北、由珍珠泉、芙蓉泉、王府池等泉水汇成、湖面46.5公顷、出小清河流入渤海。沿湖楼台亭阁、水榭长廊、参差有致、有"四面鲜花三面柳、一城山色半城湖"的佳丽景色。

Qingdao, a modern city, is a well-known summer resort.

青岛是一个现代化城市，举世闻名的避暑胜地。青岛三面环海，一面通陆，尤其是前海沿儿一带，风景秀丽，令人陶醉。

The Bund in Shanghai is located on the west bank of the Huangpu River. As early as in the 1930s, it was an economic, trade and financial center of the Far East. Nowadays, it is still the center of Shanghai's economy.

上海外滩位于黄浦江西岸，与浦东区隔水相望。早在三十年代这里就是远东经济、贸易、金融中心，至今仍是上海市的经济贸易繁华区。

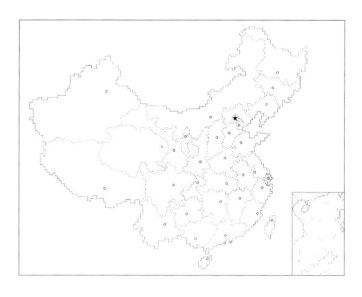

Shanghai Municipality is located at the mouth of the Yangtze River by the East Sea. Famous buildings include the Jade Buddha Temple, Jing'an Temple and Yuyuan Garden, one of the most famous gardens in southern China, where towers, terraces and pavilions are in harmony. The Central Lake Pavilion, Nine-Zigzag Bridge and Lotus-Flower Pond are all attractive spots in the garden.

上海市位于东海之滨，长江三角洲的东端。这里有玉佛寺、静安寺等古建名刹。江南名园之一的豫园也座落于此，楼台亭阁，浑然一体，湖心亭、九曲桥、荷花池各展风韵。假山重峦迭嶂，奇洞幽谷静谧，是上海市的重要景区之一。

Yuyuan Garden, a classical park in Shanghai, is famous for its Nine-Zigzag Bridge.

豫园是上海市的一处古典式的公园，园内有一座闻名中外的九曲桥，人行其上，可以在不同角度观赏风景，大大增加了视野的空间感。

Nanpu Bridge is located in the south of Shanghai. In the spring of 1990, the Shanghai Municipal Government announced the opening of the Pudong Economic and Technological Development Zone.

南浦大桥位于上海市南。1990年春，上海市政府宣布开放浦东以来，浦东新区的建设发展得很快。

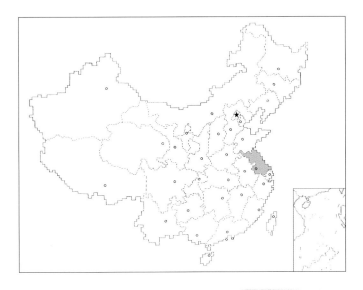

Jiangsu Province is located on the lower reaches of the Yangtze River, with the Yellow Sea to the east. Nanjing, capital of the province, is famous for Sun Yat-sen's Mausoleum, the pioneer of the Chinese revolution. In addition, the gardens in Suzhou, the Taihu Lake in Wuxi, the Golden Hill in Zhenjiang and Tangcheng in Yangzhou present beautiful natural pictures.

江苏省位于长江下游，东滨黄海。南京市的中山陵是革命先驱孙中山的陵墓，傍山而建，由南向北，逐级升高，最后是祭堂和墓室。祭堂中央有孙中山的石雕坐像，宁静肃穆。另外，苏州的园林、无锡的太湖、镇江的金山、扬州的唐城等，组成了一幅山外有山，湖外有湖的天然图画。

Sun Yat-sen's Mausoleum, located in the eastern suburbs of Nanjing, capital of Jiangsu Province, is the tomb of Dr. Sun Yat-sen, a revolutionary pioneer in modern Chinese history. It was constructed in 1926 and completed in 1929. The corpse of Sun Yat-sen was then moved here from the Temple of Azure Clouds in Beijing on June 1, 1929.

中山陵是孙中山先生的陵墓，位于南京市东郊紫金山中部。1926年开始兴建。1929年落成，同年六月一日孙中山遗体由北京碧云寺移此安葬。紫金山风景秀丽，中山陵气势磅礴，具有民族式的风格。

Wangshiyuan Garden in Suzhou was first constructed in the Southern Song Dynasty (1127-1279), and reconstructed in the reign of Emperor Qianlong (1736-1796). The garden is in the style of traditional aristocratic courtyards.

网师园位于苏州市葑门十全街，始建于南宋(1127-1279)，原建为万卷堂，多年后荒废，乾隆年间重建，称网师园。此园面积不大，但保持着旧时家族的宅院特点。布局大胆，充分利用水的效果，使景物相互衬托，浑为一体，格外幽雅。

　　枫桥位于苏州市阊门外十里的枫桥镇，创建于唐代。此桥因唐代诗人张继《枫桥夜泊》诗而闻名，故南北游客经由此处无不憩宿。自张继诗以后题咏枫桥的诗篇不胜枚举，但，唯独张继的诗最好，正如明代诗人高启在诗中写到："画枫三百映江城，诗里枫桥独有名"。

Fengqiao Bridge, located in Fengqiao Town, Suzhou, was first constructed in the Tang Dynasty (618-907). It became famous for a poem titled Staying at Fengqiao by Night written by Zhang Ji of the Tang Dynasty.

Taihu Lake is located in the southwest of Wuxi, Jiangsu Province. There are many scenic spots here, including Evergreen Hall, Yuantouzhu Island and Chenglan Hall. The park lies in front of a hill and by the river where one may view the scenery of Taihu Lake from different angles.

太湖位于无锡市西南向，这里有长春亭、诵芬堂、鼋头诸、澄澜堂等古典建筑群。其特点是以天然风光为主，园林布局依山傍水，可从不同的角度观赏万顷太湖风景。

The Narrow West Lake, located in the western suburbs of Yangzhou, Jiangsu Province, has been a famous scenic spot since ancient times. Compared with the West Lake in Hangzhou, Zhejiang Province, the lake is slimmer and more elegant, hence the name. On the banks of the lake, there are Green Poplar Village, Big Rainbow Bridge, Small Golden Hill and Fishing Terrace, presenting a fine landscape picture.

瘦西湖位于扬州市西郊、六朝以来即为风景胜地。因此湖与杭州西湖相比，另有一种清瘦秀丽的特点，故称瘦西湖。沿湖畔有绿杨村、大虹桥、小金山、钓鱼台等建筑、犹如一幅山水画卷。

Jinshan (Gold Hill) Temple is located on Jinshan Hill in Zhenjiang, Jiangsu Province. It was first constructed in the Eastern Jin Dynasty (317-420), with the original name of Cherish the Heart Temple. In the Tang Dynasty (618-907), gold was mined from the hill, hence the name. Later, it was named Dragon Tour Temple by Emperor Zhenzong of the Song Dynasty (960-1279) and Jiangtianchan Temple by Emperor Kangxi of the Qing Dynasty (1644-1911). The temple's buildings include Keeping Clouds Pavilion, Big and Small Goddess of Mercy Pavilion, and Seven-Peak Pavilion.

金山寺位于镇江市的金山上，始建于东晋(317-420)，原名泽心寺，唐代因开山得金，从此即通称金山寺。宋真宗天禧年间，因梦游金山寺，赐名龙游寺，清康熙南巡时赐名江天禅寺。庙宇依山势而造，筑有留云阁、七峰亭、妙高台等联缀山腰，使山与寺混为一体，独具风格。

Water townships are special scenes in southern China. Residential houses in Suzhou and Wuxi are built along rivers, forming a unique living style.

水乡风光是江南的一大景观，尤其苏州无锡一带，村庄民舍沿河而筑，形成了"半壁绿野半壁水，跨桥横渡两岸亲"的独特风格。这里不仅水乡风景自然幽美，而且交通运输也极为方便。

Anhui Province is located in the northwest of Central East China, with the Yangtze River and the Huaihe River passing through it. The major scenic spots in the province include Mount Huangshan and Jiuhua Mountain. Mount Huangshan is a well-known tourist destination, attractive for its weird pine trees, exotic stones and sea of clouds. Jiuhua Mountain is one of the four famous Buddhist shrines in China, and the God of the Earth is worshiped there.

安徽省位于中国华东地区的西北部、兼跨长江、淮河流域。安徽省的主要景区是黄山与九华山。黄山是驰名中外的旅游胜地，这里有奇松、怪石、云海三绝之说。九华山是中国佛教四大名山之一，供奉有地藏王的主要道场。

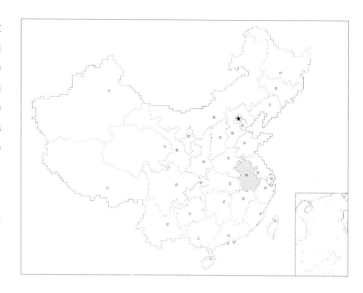

Guest Greeting Pine is located to the east of Jade Screen Tower and on top of Lord of Wisdom Cave. The pine tree growing from a rock is said to be over 1,000 years old. It is considered the eldest of the ten famous pine trees on Mount Huangshan. One of its branches looks like the extended hand of a host greeting guests coming from afar.

迎客松位于玉屏楼东、文殊洞顶。古松破石而出，枝干苍劲、形态幽美、寿逾千年、世称黄山十大名松之冠。一枝长了低垂文殊洞口，恰似好客的主人伸手迎接八方来客。

65

The peaks in the west of Mount Huangshan are called Twin Bamboo Shoots
Peak, Stone Bed Peak, Knife Peak, and Flying Here Peak.

　　西海群峰位于黄山西部，是黄山风景最秀丽的部分。挺立的山峰，如无数利剑
直插云霄，知名者有双笋峰、石床峰、尖刀峰、飞来峰等。每当云雾萦绕，层层迭
迭的峰峦时隐时现，酷似一幅淡墨图画。

Lotus Peak is the highest peak on Mount Huangshan, at 1,860 meters above sea level.

莲花峰位于黄山中部、海拔一千八百六十米、是黄山最高峰。峻峭高耸、气魄雄伟、每当云海出现、波澜壮阔、一望无际、千条深谷、万道山梁、淹没在云涛雾浪里、俨若一朵初开的新莲、仰天怒放。

Monkey Viewing the Sea, located on the top of Lion Peak, is another scenic spot on Mount Huangshan. The rock looks like a stone monkey gazing over the sea of clouds, hence the name.

猴子观海是黄山一大景观，位于狮子峰顶，因巧石形若石猴而故名。宿夜初晴，云铺深壑，形似汪洋一片，风吹云动，波涛汹涌，神如猴子观海。

Double Scissors Peak is in the west of Mount Huangshan. The sea of clouds emerges at all seasons of the year due to the high peaks, deep valleys, dense forests and abundant rainfall.

双剪峰属黄山西海景区，这里因山多峰高，谷深林密，以及雨水充沛等自然条件所致，一年四季均有云海出现。若遇寒风袭来，浓云雾凇交加，奇松怪石相依，可称黄山的绝妙胜景。

Jiuhua Mountain, located in the southwest of Qingyang County, Anhui Province, is one of the four famous Buddhist shrines in China. Zhiyuan Temple, first constructed between 1522 and 1566, was then renovated and reconstructed in the Qing Dynasty (1644-1911). It is the largest temple on the mountain.

九华山是中国佛教四大名山之一，位于安徽青阳县西南。祇园寺始建于明嘉靖年间(1522-1566)，清代几经重修、重建、规模为该山寺院之冠。

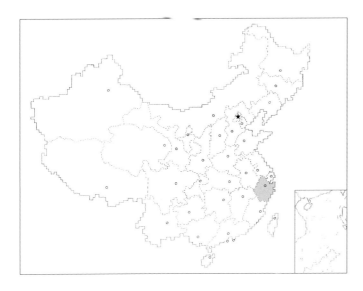

Zhejiang Province is located in the center of Central East China, by the East Sea. The West Lake is the most famous tourist resort. In addition, "Autumn Moon on the Tranquil Lake," "Snow on the Broken Bridge," "Orioles Singing in the Willows," and "Lotus in the Courtyard" are all scenic spots here. Putuo Mountain on the Zhoushan Peninsula is one of the four famous Buddhist shrines in China.

浙江省位于中国华东地区中部、东海之滨。这里著名的风景区是杭州市的西湖。平湖秋月、断桥残雪、柳浪闻莺、曲院风荷，各有特色。舟山群岛中的普陀山，是中国佛教四大名山之一。

The Autumn Moon on the Tranquil Lake, located in the west of the White Dam of the West Lake in Hangzhou, Zhejiang Province, is one of the ten famous scenes on the West Lake. When the moon rises on an autumn night, the lake is calm and reflects the brightness of the moon.

平湖秋月在杭州西湖白堤两端。前临外湖、水面开阔、在皓月当空的秋夜、湖平如镜、清辉如泻。前人有诗云："万顷湖平长似镜，四时月好最宜秋"。故平湖秋月，是西湖的十景之一。

Baoshu (Bless and Protect Hongshu) Pagoda, located on Gem Hill in Hangzhou, Zhejiang Province, was first built between 968 and 976. It is said that when Taizu, the first emperor of the Northern Song Dynasty (960-1127), unified the country, he called Qian Hongshu, king of Wuyue, to Nanjing, the capital. Qian's mother built the pagoda in an attempt to ensure the safe return of her son.

保俶塔在杭州市宝石山上。原名应天塔、建于北宋开宝(968-976)年间。据传，北宋统一后，太祖召吴越国王钱弘俶进京，其母舅吴延爽发愿建造此塔，祈求弘俶平安归来，故称保俶塔。塔身秀挺、卓立山巅、未近西湖先见此塔，西湖一景。

Hangzhou Botanical Garden, located to the northwest of the West Lake, integrates natural scenery, a garden-like atmosphere, and science and education.

　　杭州植物园位于西湖西北面、地处双峰插云与玉泉观鱼之间的皇陵地带。园内起伏不平，造林布局采用了自然风景式，富有科学内容，又具有公园外貌，是西湖著名园林风景之一。

Liuhe (Six Harmonies) Pagoda is located on Crescent Hill by the Qiantang River, south of Hangzhou. The pagoda, built by Qian Hongshu, King of Wuyue, in 970, was destroyed in 1121. The present brick-structure pagoda was built in 1153.

　　六和塔位于杭州市城南钱塘江边的月轮山上。北宋开宝三年（970）吴越王钱弘俶为镇江潮而建，宣和三年（1121）毁于兵火。现存砖构塔身系南宋绍兴二十三年（1153）重建。登塔临窗，江山俊秀，尽收眼底。

Lingyin Temple, located on Lingyin Mountain, northwest of the West Lake, with Lingquan Spring and The Peak That Flew Here in its front, is one of the ten famous Zen temples in China. It was first constructed in 327, and was expanded twice later. At one time, there were nine towers, 18 pavilions, 72 halls, 1,200 rooms and 2,000 monks.

灵隐寺是我国佛教禅宗十刹之一、位于西湖西北灵隐山麓、前临冷泉、面对飞来峰。东晋咸和初年（327）兴建、五代吴越国时曾两次扩建、当时有九楼、十八阁、七十二殿、僧徒二千人、房屋一千二百余间、极盛一时。寺内古木苍郁、遮天盖日、清幽静谧。

Bamboo Path is located in the west of Wuyun Mountain, near Hangzhou, 20 kilometers from the West Lake, and is one of the 18 scenic spots of the West Lake. The dense bamboo forests, the green mountain and the clear brook form a beautiful picture.

云栖竹径位于杭州市五云山之西的山坞内、距西湖二十公里许。沿坞修竹茂林、溪水澄湖、云栖竹经称为西湖十八景之一。昔人有诗曰："万千竿竹浓荫密、流水青山如画图"、道出了云栖的特色。

Putuo Mountain, an island of the Zhoushan Archipelago in Zhejiang Province, is one of the four famous Buddhist shrines in China, and the place of enlightenment of the Goddess of Mercy. There are over 20 scenic spots on the island, of which Puji Temple, Fayu Temple and Huiji Temple are famous.

普陀山是中国佛教四大名山之一，是浙江省舟山群岛中的一个小岛，世称为观世音道场。岛上有风景点二十余处，其中普济寺、法雨寺、慧济寺三大寺庙最为突出。每当风和日丽登上佛顶山，远眺天际、海外海、天外天、岛外岛、山外山的宏伟景色，美不胜收。

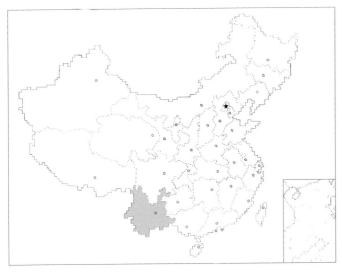

Yunnan Province is located in the far southwest of China, neighboring Vietnam, Laos and Myanmar. The Grand View Tower, Yuantong Temple, Black Dragon Pool and Green Lake are famous tourism spots in Kunming, capital of Yunnan. Three pagodas of Chongsheng Temple in Dali City and the Flying Dragon White Pagoda in Jinghong County are exquisite. The Stone Forest in Lunan County and the rock paintings in Cangyuan County are unique sights.

云南省位于中国西南地区南部边境，南部和西部与越南、老挝、缅甸三国接壤。昆明市的大观楼、圆通寺、黑龙潭、翠湖等，垂柳拂波，楼台倒映。大理市的崇圣三塔、景洪县的飞龙白塔，精巧维妙，各有千秋。路南县的石林，沧源县的岩画，更是一绝。

Greenery Lake is located in Kunming, capital of Yunnan Province. In Emperor Kangxi's reign between 1662 and 1722, a pavilion was constructed in the middle of the lake with lotus flowers and willow trees around.

翠湖位于云南省昆明市区内，清初吴三桂在南方称王割据，填湖近半，建造王府。吴死后其孙吴世潘称帝，年号洪化，称府为洪化府。康熙年间，就湖中小岛建湖心亭。湖岸垂柳拂动，池中莲花满塘，时时有花，处处有景。

Yuantong Temple, located in Kunming, on Yuantong Street and at the foot of Yuantong Mountain, is composed of Wonderland Archway, Pentagon Pavilion, Yuantong Hall, and the zigzagging corridor to Water Pavilion.

圆通寺位于昆明市内、前临圆通街、后接圆通山。寺由圆通胜境坊、八角亭、圆通宝殿、水榭曲廊等建筑组成。是昆明一大胜境。

The Stone Forest, located in the Lunan Yi Autonomous County of Yunnan Province, is composed of fantastic stone peaks and pillars.

石林位于云南省路南彝族自治县内。这里群山壁立，千嶂迭翠，巨大的石峰、石柱拔地而起，直刺青天，犹如一片莽莽森林，故名石林。

The Three Pagodas at Chongsheng Temple are located in Dali County, Yunnan Province. The three brick pagodas are erected on the top of Cangshan Hill and by the Erhai Sea. The bigger pagoda was built between 824 and 839, while the two smaller ones were constructed in the Five Dynasties (907-960).

崇圣寺三塔位于大理县城西崇圣寺内。三座砖塔鼎立于苍山之麓，洱海之滨。大塔方形，中空，名千寻塔。建筑年代众说纷纭，以建于南诏保和时期为是（824-839）。两小塔为实心、八角形，建于五代（907-960），气势雄伟。

The Flying Dragon White Pagodas, located on Manfeilong Hill in Jinghong County, Yunnan Province, are nine big and small white pagodas. The white pagodas, also known as "Bamboo Pagodas," constructed in 1204, are buildings of the Lesser Vehicle.

飞龙白塔位于景洪县大勐笼的曼飞龙后山上。塔群有大小九塔组成、塔身刷成白色、苑如玉笋破土而出、故有笋塔之称。为青砖结构、建于傣历五百六十五年（1204）、系小乘佛教建筑。

Black Dragon Pool is located at the foot of the Elephant Hill in the Naxi Autonomous County, Lijiang City, Yunnan Province. The snow-capped Jade Dragon Peak is reflected in the pool.

黑龙潭位于丽江纳西族自治县象山脚下。潭面宽阔、碧水澄浏、玉龙雪峰倒映其间、堤上绿树翁郁、景色一览无余。

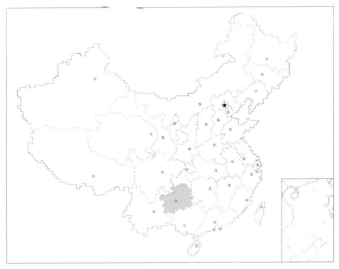

Guizhou Province is located in the east of the Yunnan-Guizhou Plateau. The Wenchang Pavilion, Jiaxiu Tower, Flower Brook and Holy Spring are famous scenic spots in Guiyang, capital of Guizhou. Red Maple Lake in Qingzhen County, Black Dragon Cave in Zhenyuan County, White Cloud Mountain in Changshun County and the Huangguoshu Waterfall in Zhenning County are ideal tourist destinations.

贵州省位于云贵高原东部。文昌阁、甲秀楼、花溪、圣泉等，都是贵阳市的著名风光。清镇县的红枫湖、镇远县的青龙洞、长顺县的白云山、镇宁县的黄果树瀑布等，霞雾生烟，悠然可见，诗情画意，令人流连。

The Underground Park, also known as the "Southern Suburbs Park," is located by the Xiaoche River, south of Guiyang City, capital of Guizhou Province. This karst cave is thought to have been formed two million years ago.

地下公园也称南郊公园，位于贵州省贵阳南小车河畔。此处荒山一座，山下游亭屹立，奇特的地下公园即由此进洞。据考，溶洞形成于二百万年以前。洞中石笋、石柱、石花、石幔维妙维肖，引人入胜。

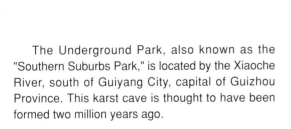

Yuping (Jade Screen) Scenery is located in Yuping County,
Guizhou Province, where the river, flowers and old trees form a
harmonious and natural picture.

玉屏风光位于贵州省玉屏县境内。这里水绕花岭、山抱苗寨、
繁花似锦、古树葱茏，一幅清晰和谐、争奇斗胜的自然画卷。

Huangguoshu Waterfall is located on the Baishui River in the Buyi and Miao Autonomous County, Guizhou Province. It has a drop of 74 meters.

黄果树瀑布位于镇宁布依族、苗族自治县的白水河上。飞流奔腾、泻崖而下，落差达 74 米、水势汹涌、波浪滔滔，形成了黄果树瀑布。

Chongqing Municipality is located on the upper reaches of the Yangtze River in the southeast of Sichuan Province. Famous scenic spots include the South and North hot springs, Laojun Cave, Arhat Temple and Jinyun Mountain, serving as ideal summer resorts.

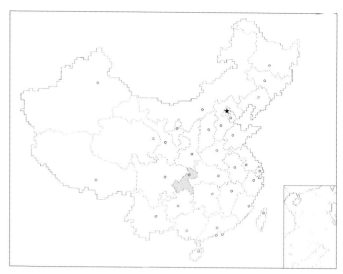

　　重庆市位于四川省东南部、长江上游。这里的白公馆、渣滓洞都是国民党军统局的监狱，屠杀过众多革命者。著名的风景区有南温泉、北温泉、老君洞、罗汉寺、缙云山等，林木葱郁、浓荫蔽日，山洞流水与林中鸣鸟相互回应，别有情趣。是避暑及游览胜地。

Shibao Village, located in the east of Zhongxian County, attracts tourists by its high hills, zigzagging streams, green pine trees and bamboo, and nine-floor towers.

　　石宝寨位于长江畔的忠县以东。孤峰突起、直升凌空，山下溪水环绕，山上松竹苍翠。寨中楼阁九层、重檐高耸，点翠流丹，四时游人不绝。

The Qutang Gorge, one of the famous Three Gorges on the Yangtze River, stretches from Baidi City in Fengjie County in the west to Daxi Town in Wushan County in the east, lengthening a total of eight kilometers.

瞿塘峡是长江三峡之一。西起奉节县的白帝城，东迄巫山县的大溪镇，全长约八公里，以峰奇险峻而著称。两岸丛山入云，江水波涛汹涌，令人惊心动魄。

Sichuan Province, located on the upper reaches of the Yangtze River, has the most cultural relics and places of natural scenery in China. Du Fu's Thatched Cottage, Zhuge Liang's Memorial Hall, Overlooking the River Tower and the mosque are famous scenic spots in Chengdu, capital of the province. The Yangtze River, the Giant Buddha at Leshan, the stone grottoes at Dazu, the scenery of the Jiuzhaigou Nature Reserve are other famous tourist destinations in Sichuan. Mount Emei is one of the four famous Buddhist shrines in China.

四川省位于长江上游，是文物古迹与自然风光最多的省份。成都市的杜甫草堂、武侯祠、望江楼、清真寺等，花木葱郁、重峦迭翠。省内还有著名的长江三峡、乐山大佛、大足石窟、九寨风光、景色秀丽、引人入胜。峨眉山是中国佛教四大名山之一。

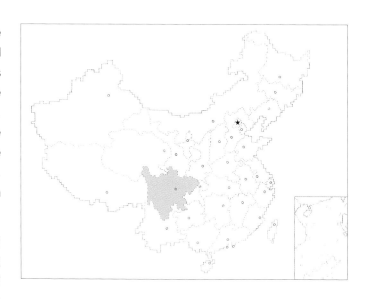

Du Fu's Thatched Cottage, located in the western suburbs of Chengdu, capital of Sichuan Province, is the former dwelling of Du Fu (712-770), a noted poet of the Tang Dynasty (618-907). It was first built as a memorial hall in the Northern Song Dynasty (960-1127) and was renovated in the Yuan, Ming and Qing dynasties (1279-1911).

杜甫草堂位于四川省成都市西郊，是唐代诗人杜甫（712-770）故宅。北宋元丰年间始建茅屋立祠、元、明、清历代均曾改建修葺。梅园南林、翠竹千竿、溪水小桥、交错庭间，为故宅增添了无限诗情画意。

Mount Emei, located in the western part of Emei County, Sichuan Province, is one of the four famous Buddhist shrines in China. Ten-Thousand Buddha Peak, the highest peak of the mountain, is 3,099 meters above sea level. There are 100 big and small temples altogether on the mountain.

峨眉山是中国佛教四大名山之一。位于峨眉县城西。主峰万佛顶海拔三千零九十九米，山脉峰峦起伏、雄秀幽奇，素有"峨眉天下秀"之美誉。这里有大小寺庙近百座。

Jiuzhaigou Nature Reserve, located in Nanping County, Sichuan Province, is a 40-kilometer-long valley on Minshan Mountain. It gained its name from nine Tibetan villages there. Enclosed by mountains and dense forests, the valley is famous for over 100 big and small lakes.

九寨沟位于四川省南坪县境内，是岷山山脉的一条山谷地，长约四十公里，因有九个藏民村寨面得名。四周群峰耸峙、森林密布，，河谷有大小湖泊一百多处，湖水碧蓝，瀑布腾空，颇为壮观。

Conch Gully is located in Nanping County, Sichuan Province. There are dozens of peaks capped by snow the whole year round.

海螺沟位于四川南坪县。沟中地僻人稀、风景特异、有"童话世界"之誉。有雪峰数十座、积雪终年不化、在阳光的照射下、呈现出各种颜色、绚丽夺目。

Huanglong Nature Reserve, located in Huanglong Town, north of the Songpan County, Sichuan Province, has thick forests and numerous ponds.

黄龙位于四川松潘县城北黄龙乡。四周林木繁多、宛若碧海。大小水池重迭、数以万计、状若梯湖、水色斑烂、蔚为壮观。

Wolong Gully, located on the east bank of the Mingjiang River, Wenchuan County, Sichuan Province, is situated between the Sichuan Basin and the Qinghai-Tibet Plateau. It is rich in animal and plant resources.

卧龙沟位于汶川县岷江东岸。卧龙沟地处四川盆地和青藏高原的过度地带、动植物资源极为丰富。白雪皑皑、重峦迭障、景色秀丽，引人入胜。

The Giant Buddha on Leshan Mountain is located on the western cliff of Lingyun Mountain, at the juncture of the Minjiang, Qingyi and Dadu rivers. Work on the statue started in 713, and was completed in 803. It is the largest stone-carved Buddha in the world, with a height of 71 meters.

乐山大佛位于长江畔乐山市东凌云山的西壁上，岷江、青衣江、大渡河三江合流处。大佛依凌云山栖鸾断崖凿成一尊弥勒坐像，故又名凌云大佛。大佛是唐开元年(713)，名僧海通创建，贞元十九年(803)完成，前后工程进行了约九十年的时间。佛高七十一米，是世界上最大的石刻佛像。

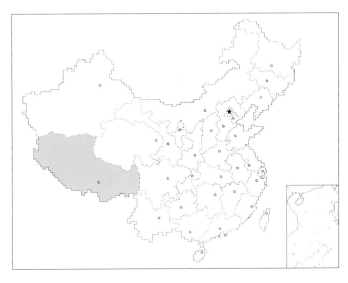

The Tibet Autonomous Region is located on the Qinghai-Tibet Plateau, known as the "Roof of the World," in the southwest of China, neighboring India, Nepal, Sikkim, Bhutan and Myanmar in the west and south. The Jokhang Monastery is located in the center of Lhasa,as is the Potala Palace, illustrating the essence of ancient Tibetan architecture. In addition, Tibet boasts many places of cultural interest and natural scenery.

西藏自治区位于中国西南边疆号称"世界屋脊"的青藏高原之上，西部和南部与印度、尼泊尔、锡金、不丹、缅甸等国相邻。著名的大昭寺就在拉萨市中心，布达拉宫建于山上，是中国宫堡式的建筑群，也是藏族古建筑艺术的精华。此外，西藏还有众多文物古迹和自然风光，是中外旅游胜地。

The Jokhang Monastery, located in the center of Lhasa, was constructed in the mid 7th century. It contains statues of Sakyamuni, Songtsan Gambo and Princess Wencheng.

大昭寺位于拉萨市中心。建于公元七世纪中叶，后经历代修缮增建，形成庞大的建筑群。大殿正中有释迦牟尼像，西侧配殿是吐蕃赞普松赞干布和文成公主塑像，仪态生动大方。

The Potala Palace, located in Lhasa, in the Tibet Autonomous Region, is the most famous palace complex in China. Its name means "Holy Land of Buddhism" in Sanskrit. It has been renovated and expanded many times since it was first built during the Tang Dynasty (618-907).

布达拉宫位于西藏拉萨市内，是我国著名的宫殿建筑群。布达拉宫梵语意为"佛教圣地"。相传公元七世纪时，吐蕃赞普松赞干布与唐联姻，为迎娶文成公主在此建室。后世屡有修筑，始具今日规模。

The splendid Golden Knob Group of the Potala Palace marks the halls containing the funerary stupas of the 5th, 7th, 9th, 10th and 13th Dalai Lamas.

布达拉宫金顶群是表达五世、七世、九世、十世、十三世达赖喇嘛灵塔殿金顶和圣观音主殿金顶的，通过这些建筑，组成了一个奇特的金碧辉煌的金顶群。

This statue of the Buddha of Future, built by the order of the 8th Dalai Lama in 1800, is made of gilded copper.

弥勒菩萨像是用铜质镀金的、是寝宫甘丹平措内主要所依。1800年八世达赖喇嘛降白嘉措建造。

The West Hall of the Red Palace is the location of the throne of the 6th Dalai Lama. There are many exotic engravings on the pillars and beams of the hall.

西大殿位于红宫西有寂圆满大殿内，设有六世达赖喇嘛仓央嘉措坐的宝座。殿内柱梁上有各种奇异的雕刻，用四种珍宝涂底色，色彩鲜艳而壮观。

Palkor Monastery, located in Gyantse County, was constructed in the early 15th century. There is a Buddhist pagoda in the monartery where exquisite sculptures and frescoes are preserved.

　　白居寺位于江孜县城区。十五世纪初叶由江孜地方封建势力、饶丹贡桑帕和喇嘛教僧人克主杰共同筹建、寺内建有佛塔一座，塔内保存有精美的雕塑和壁画。

Bomi is one of the sacred spots of Buddhism, attracting pilgrims from all over the world every year.

波密风光山水并胜，景色宜人。传说此湖是王母居住的瑶池，是著名的佛教圣地之一，每年前往朝拜的国内外教徒甚多。

Guangdong Province is located in the south of China. Famous scenic spots in Guangzhou, capital of the province, include Five Rams Hill, Zhenhai Tower, Liuhua Lake, Luogang Cave and the Sun Yat-sen Memorial Hall. In addition, Seven-Star Rock, and Water Moon Palace in Zhaoqing are also worthy visiting.

广东省位于中国南部。广州市内的主要风景有五羊山、镇海楼、流花湖、萝岗洞等、以及红柱黄墙、庄严肃穆的中山纪念堂、都是游览的好去处。肇庆市的七星岩、水月宫等景区、三面环水、银湖黛峰、回廊曲折、交相辉映。

Five Rams Hill, located in Yuexiu Park in Guangzhou, Guangdong Province, is so called because of the stone statue of five rams. According to legend, they saved the local people from famine.

五羊山在广州市越秀公园内。因山顶矗立着五羊石像而得名。传说周夷王时、有五个仙人骑着五只衔着六支谷穗的羊降临此处、把谷穗赠给州人、永无饥荒。仙人言毕隐去、羊化为石、故塑五羊为志。

Sun Yat-sen Memorial Hall, located on Yuexiu Hill in Guangzhou, was built to commemorate Dr. Sun Yat-sen, the great revolutionary pioneer in modern Chinese history. The construction started in January 1929, and was completed in October 1931.

中山纪念堂位于广州市越秀山南麓，为纪念我国近代伟大的民主革命家孙中山而兴建。1929年1月奠基、1931年10月落成。堂前塑有孙中山钢像，是广州人民集会的重要场所。

Guifeng Hill is a general term for the hills in the north of Xinhui County, near Xinhui Labor University. The major scenic spot is Jade Lake, covering 80,000 square meters.

圭峰山是新会县城北诸山之总称。游览区主要在新会劳动大学附近。这里有玉湖，占地八万平方米，环湖有美丽的丛林，湖中建有楼阁亭台，长桥接岸，水清如玉，是新会县的游览胜地。

Seven-Star Rock is located in the north of Zhaoqing City, Guangdong Province. It is composed of seven precipitous limestone rocks, in a formation like that of the Big Dipper.

七星岩又名星湖，位于广东肇庆市北，由七座陡峭的石灰岩组成，布列似北斗七星，故名。其风景以湖岩石洞而取胜，并有"七岩、八洞、五湖、六岗"之称。有桂林之山、杭州之水的美誉。

Shenzhen Aquatic Amusement ▷ Park is a seaside park that attracts many tourists during holidays.

深圳海上世界是一个海滨式的公园，也是深圳人游览度假的好去处。

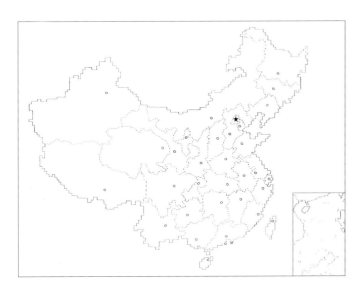

The Hong Kong Special Administrative Region is located in the far south of Guangdong Province, neighboring Sanmen Island in the east, the Zhujiang River in the west and the Wanshan Peninsula in the south. It is an international hub of commerce and the southern gateway to China. Hong Kong has a prosperous economy, mild climate and beautiful scenery.

香港特别行政区位于广东省最南部、东临三门岛、西依珠江口、南濒万山群岛。它地居世界航道的要冲，并扼中国华南的门户。这里经济繁荣、贸易昌盛、气候宜人、风景秀美。

There are many parks in Hong Kong, which are very popular at holiday times.

香港境内有很多公园绿地，大多秀丽怡人。每当休闲之日，总要引来很多游人驻足其间。在众多游人中最惹人注目的当属一对对情侣和年轻的夫妇们。

◁ Taiping Mountain is the highest peak in Hong Kong, 544 meters above sea level. It gives a panoramic view of Victoria Harbor, the Kowloon Peninsula and the South China Sea.

太平山是香港第一高峰，海拔544米。在山顶之上可俯瞰维多利亚港、九龙南部及南中国海的壮丽景色。图为太平山下的繁华景象。此处也是俯瞰夜景的绝妙之处。

The Guangxi Zhuang Autonomous Region ▷ is located in the southwest of China, bordering on the Beibu Gulf in the south and Vietnam in the southwest. The 40-kilometers stretch of the Lijiang River from Guilin to Yangshuo County is the major scenic spot of the region, well known for its exotic peaks, beautiful rivers, green bamboos and wide fields.

广西壮族自治区位于中国中南地区的西南部、南濒北部湾、西南与越南为邻。该自治区的主要风景当首推漓江风光，在桂林市至阳朔的的四十公里间，山峰奇特，秀水潆洄，茂林翠竹，田野似锦，真是一江流水千幅画、无限优美。

Dayushan is the largest island in Hong Kong. There is a famous giant Buddha on the island, 26.4 meters high, making it the tallest bronze sitting Buddha in the world. The Lotus Temple is only a few hundred meters from the Buddha.

大屿山是香港境内最大的岛屿。岛上有著名的天坛大佛，佛通高26.4米，是世界上最大的户外青铜坐佛。距大佛前数百米是佛门胜地宝莲禅寺。

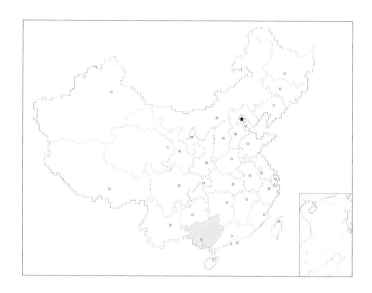

Guilin, located in the northeast of the Guangxi Zhuang Autonomous Region, is famous not only for its unique scenery but also for its cultural relics, including 2,000 stone carvings.

　桂林市是一座历史名城，位于广西壮族自治区东北部。这里山水清幽，风光秀丽，中唐后即成为风景胜地。除自然风景外，还有很多文物古迹，仅石刻艺术就有二千余件，遍布各风景点。自古就有"桂林山水甲天下"的美誉，是我国著名的风景游览区。

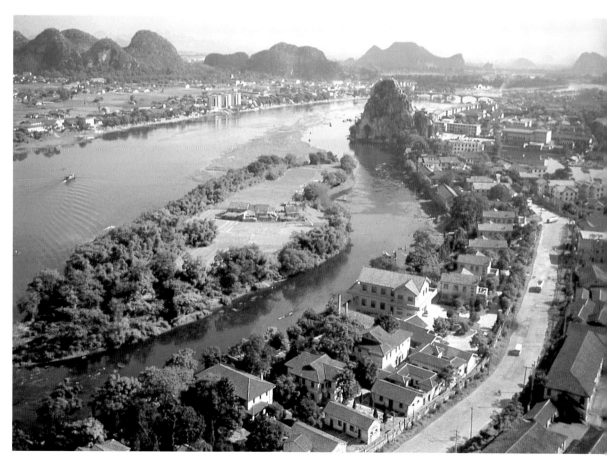

The Lijiang River, originating in Xing'an County, northeast of Guilin, passes through Guilin and Yangshuo, and enters the Xijiang River at Wuzhou. Cruises on the river from Guilin to Yangshuo are popular with tourists.

　　漓江是桂林山水的重要组成部分。漓江发源于桂林东北兴安县、流经桂林、阳朔、在梧州汇入西江。漓江山水最精华的一段是桂林至阳朔、山峰奇特、秀水潆洄、真是一江流水千幅画、八方来客万家情。

The scenery on Lijiang River is like a traditional Chinese painting.

漓江风光云山万里，尤其从桂林至阳朔之间，峰峦迭影，翠竹茂林，奇山秀水，风帆渔筏，处处诗情画意，无不油然而生。

Xingping is an old town in the north of Yangshuo County, the middle part of the Lijiang River, serving as the highlight of Lijiang Landscape.

兴坪风光位于阳朔县城北、是漓江中段的一个古镇。这里山峰密集、青山浮水、古有阳朔山水在兴坪之说。镇前有榕潭、潭水碧澄、深不见底、泊船良港、樯桅林立、沙湾夕照、宛如水上市镇。

Yangshuo scenery is located in the north of Yangshuo County with elegant hills, precipitous rocks, caves and zigzagging rivers.

　　阳朔风光位于阳朔县城北。山峰峻秀苍翠，石壁嶙峋峭拔，洞穴千姿百态，江水清沏迂回。古人诗云："阳川百里尽是画，碧莲峰下有人家"，秀丽的阳朔风光，处处令人神往。

Scholar's Page-Boy Hill, located in the south of Yangshuo, is compared to a slim and elegant girl.

　　书童山位于阳朔县城南，山呈圆形，挺拔峻秀，直冲太空。周围彩壁如屏，山顶绿树成林。好似一个端庄的少女，亭亭玉立，对江自照，山影江心，清奇无比。

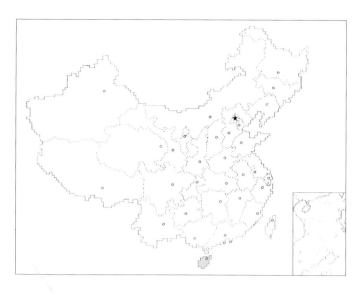

Hainan Province, the largest island in the South China Sea, is famous for many scenic spots, including Five-Finger Hill, Dropping Brush Cave, Deer Looking Back, and Edge of Heaven and Corner of the Sea.

海南省位于中国南海，是南海诸岛中最大的一个岛屿。这里的著名风景有五指山、落笔洞、鹿回头、天涯海角等。此处，海天一色，蔚蓝皎洁，奇石磊磊，雪浪翻花，景色十分壮观。

Yuelong Bay on Hainan Island is a sequestered spot sheltered by coconut trees.

牙笼湾是海南岛的游览胜地，这里椰林茂密、幽雅洁静、可以尽览海上风光。

The scenic spot named "Edge of the Heaven and Corner of the Sea" is located in Sanya Town.

　　天涯海角位于三亚镇。此处巨石耸立，清雍正十一年(1733)，崖州知州程哲等题刻"天涯"、"海角"、"海阔天空"、"南天一柱"等字，故称天涯海角。这里斜峙大海、乱石棋布，是海南岛的著名景区。

Coconut Forest Holiday Resort is located in Wenchang County, Hainan Province. The Wenchang County Tourism Administration has set up a folk holiday village here.

椰林度假村位于海南岛文昌县境内。这里椰林丛丛、海风习习、风光秀丽、气候宜人。为了便于群众游览南国风情，文昌县旅游局在这里修建了一个民间式的度假村、接待来往游人。

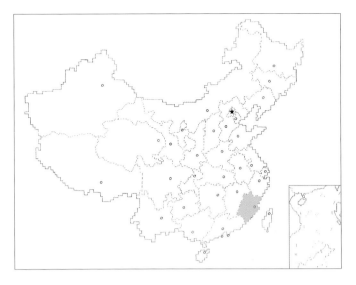

福建省位于中国华东地区的南部，东隔台湾海峡与台湾相望。该省的著名景区有武夷山、鼓浪屿、风动石、老君岩、涌泉寺、湄洲湾等。值得细述的是惠安县的惠安女，现已成为中国的一大风情，她们的服式也形成了非少数民族的民族化形式。前来观光旅游的人，络绎不绝。

Fujian Province is located in the south of Central East China, facing Taiwan across the Taiwan Strait in the east. Famous tourist spots include Wuyi Mountain, Gulangyu Island, Stone Moving with the Wind, Laojun Rock, Yongquan Temple and Meizhou Gulf. The brilliant costumes of the girls of Huian County are a special tourist attraction.

Yongquan Temple, located on the Drum Hill in the eastern suburbs of Fuzhou, capital of Fujian Province, is famous for its 18 scenic spots.

涌泉寺位于福州市东郊鼓山之上，为福州著名寺院。寺动灵源洞、听水斋一带，岩石嵯峨，摩崖密集，誉称"石鼓都会"。寺西苍松翠柏，曲径通幽，有鼓山十八景之说。

Gulangyu Island is located in the western part of Xiamen, Fujian Province, covering an area of one square kilometer. The island is known as "Garden on the Sea" and "Music Island."

　　鼓浪屿位于厦门市西、中隔七百多米的厦门海峡，全岛约一平方公里。岛上冈峦起伏、四季花香、树木葱郁，亭台楼阁，以"海上花园"或"音乐岛"而驰名中外。

湄州岛位于蒲田市湄州湾口、妈祖神祖庙座落在岛上、每年来此朝拜的海内外人士数以千计、特别是福建沿海、台、港、澳游客、终年不断、香火极为鼎盛。

妈祖庙位于湄州岛、建于宋初。开始规模不大、后经历代扩建、规模日臻雄伟、最后形成五组建筑群、十六殿堂楼阁、九十九间斋舍客房。庙宇依山相建、金碧辉煌、恰似海上龙宫。

Meizhou Island is located at the mouth of the Meizhou Gulf in Putian City, Fujian Province. The temple of the Goddess Mazu is sited on the island, attracting thousands of pilgrims, especially from Taiwan, Hong Kong and Macao, every year. The temple was first constructed in the early Song Dynasty (960-1279) and was then expanded in the following successive dynasties. There are five buildingcomplexes, with 16 halls and towers and 99 guest rooms.

The Twin Pagodas at Kaiyuan Temple are located in Quanzhou City, Fujian Province, with a distance of 200 meters in between.

开元寺双塔位于泉州市内，两塔东西对峙，相距约二百米。东塔名镇国塔，西塔名仁寿塔，两塔历经风雨仍不变形，表现了我国建筑艺术的高度成就。

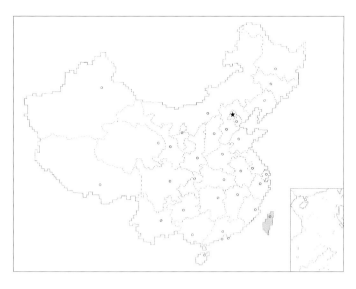

Taiwan Province is located between the East Sea and the North Sea, with the Pacific Ocean in the east. Major scenic spots are Ali Mountain and Sun and Moon Pool. It is said that one half of Half Screen Hill is on Taiwan and the other half is on China's mainland, indicating the close ties between Taiwan and the mainland.

台湾省位于中国的东海与南海之间，东临太平洋、西与福建省隔水相望。台湾的主要风景有阿里山和日月潭。传说，半屏山的一半在台湾，另一半在大陆，反映了自古以来与大陆心心相连之情。

Sun and Moon Pool, located in Nantou County, in central Taiwan, is a famous scenic spot in Taiwan Province.

日月潭是台湾省的著名风景区之一，位于台湾中部南投县丛山之中。该潭是全省最大的天然湖，湖中有一个小岛，岛北为日潭，岛南为月潭，以潭形近似日月而得名。1931年因下游山麓兴建水电站，水位提高，至此日月形状已不复存，故更名光华岛。岛上林木扶疏、翠峰环抱、明月清晖、环境幽谧，是游人观光佳地。

Ali Mountain, located to the east of Chaii, Taiwan Province, is easily reached by train. Its highest peak is 2,663 meters above sea level. The mountain is famous for its natural forests, and a 53-meter-tall juniper there is said to be over 3,000 years old.

阿里山位于台湾嘉义市东，主峰海拔二千六百六十三米，可乘小火车抵达。阿里山是台湾著名的天然森林区，古木参天，绿树葱茏，其中一株老红桧树，高约五十三米，树龄达三千余年，被称为"神木"。

Henan Province, known as the "Central Plain," is located on the middle and lower reaches of the Yellow River. Shaolin Temple, White Horse Temple, Dragon Pavilion and Tombs of the Song Dynasty are some of Henan's attractions. The Longmen Grottoes, one of the three biggest grotto complexes in China, are sited 13 kilometers south of Luoyang, capital of the province. Mount Songshan, on which there are many historical relics, is one of the five famous mountains in China.

河南省位于黄河中下游，向有"中原"之称。少林寺、白马寺、龙亭、宋陵等名胜古迹，分布各地。龙门石窟在洛阳市南十三公里处，是中国三大石窟之一。嵩山属中国五岳之一，山峦起伏，峻峰奇异，名胜古迹、星罗棋布。

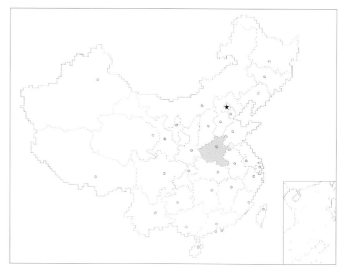

Shaolin Temple, located at the foot of Wuru Peak on Shaoshi Mountain in Henan Province, was first built in 495. In 527, an Indian monk created Zen here. Monks from the temple helped Emperor Taizong (reigned from 627 to 650) take the throne of the Tang Dynasty, and a tradition of martial arts started there which has become famous worldwide.

少林寺位于河南省少室山五乳峰下。建于北魏太和十九年(495)、孝昌三年(527)即印度僧人菩提达摩在此首创禅宗，历史上称达摩为初祖、称少林寺为祖庭。唐初少林寺和尚扶佐唐太宗(627-650在位)开国有功，从此僧徒常习拳术、禅宗和少林拳负有盛名，广为流传。

Mount Songshan, located in the northwest of Dengfeng County, Henan Province, is one of the five famous mountains in China. The pagoda on the mountain, constructed in 520, is the oldest brick Buddhist pagoda remaining in China, with a history of over 1,000 years.

嵩山是中国著名的五岳之一，位于河南登封县西北。嵩山塔寺始建于北魏正光元年(520)，是我国现存的最古老的砖砌佛塔。此塔用青砖黄泥垒砌而成，一千多年来，巍然屹立。

White Horse Temple, located in the east of Luoyang, Henan Province, and first built in 68, is said to have been the first Buddhist temple in China. Legend has it that the Buddhist scriptures were brought here on a white horse, hence the name of the temple. The Qiyun Pagoda, built in 1175 in the east of the temple, is 24 meters high.

白马寺位于洛阳市东，建于东汉永平十一年(68)，是佛教传入我国后兴建的第一座寺院。相传蔡愔、蔡景二人去西域求经，路遇来自天竺的迦叶摩腾和竺法兰二僧，用白马驮经，迎回洛阳。次年建寺以白马命名。寺东有金大定十五年(1175)建造的齐云塔，高二十四米。古刹黄墙、茂林高塔、遥相辉映。

Longmen (Dragon Gate) Grottoes, located on both banks of the Yihe River in Luoyang, Henan Province, were excavated in the period between 471 and 499. After expansion during the following 400 years, the niches now number 2,100, with 100,000 statues.

龙门石窟位于洛阳市南伊河两岸。石窟开创于北魏孝文帝(471-499)，历经东西魏至宋朝四百余年的大规模营造，两山窟龛，密似蜂窝。共计窟龛二千一百多个，造像十万余尊。

Huiyuankou (Entrance to the Garden) is located on the southern bank of the Yellow River, 18 kilometers north of Zhengzhou, capital of Henan Province. It was a pleasure garden during the Ming Dynasty (1368-1644).

花园口位于河南省 郑州市北十八公里处，紧靠黄河南岸。明吏部尚书许某在此修建花园，后河道南移、村落与花园被水吞没，成为黄河渡口、名花园口。

Dragon Pavilion, located in the northwest of Kaifeng, Henan
Province, used to be the imperial garden of an empress of the Song
Dynasty (960-1279). Prince Zhou of the Ming Dynasty (1368-1644)
used to frequent the garden. At the end of the Ming Dynasty, the
prince's garden was destroyed by a flood, leaving only the Coal Hill,
where coal used to be stored. In 1692, Longevity Pavilion was built
on the hill, where officials gathered to kowtow on the occasion of the
emperor's birthday. The hill was then renamed Dragon Pavilion Hill.

龙亭位于开封市西北隅，原为宋代皇宫后的御苑。亭下高台是明代
周王府花园中的土山，蓄放煤炭，故称煤山。明末河决城淹，王府沦没，
煤山巍峨独存，清康熙三十一年(1692)在煤山旧址建万寿亭。逢皇帝生
日，文武官吏来此朝拜，称煤山为龙亭山，故更名为龙亭。

Hubei Province is located on the middle reaches of the Yangtze River to the north of Dongting Lake. Famous scenic spots include Turtle Hill, Snake Hill, East Lake, Yellow Crane Tower, Temple of Qu Yuan and Mi Fu's Memorial Hall. Wudang Mountain, the major scenic spot in the province and one of the most famous mountains in China, has exotic peaks and precipitous valleys. The scenery is magnificent with the total length of the tour to the top measuring 60 kilometers.

湖北省位于长江中游、洞庭湖以北。该省风景区有龟山、蛇山、东湖、黄鹤楼、屈原庙、米宫祠等。武当山是中国的名山、湖北省的主要风景区、峰奇谷险、洞室幽邃、全山游程达六十公里之遥、风景极为壮观。

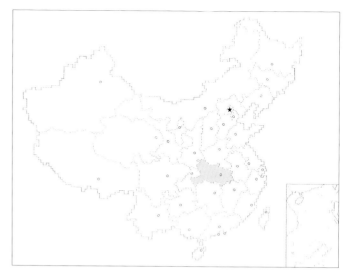

East Lake, located in the eastern suburbs of Wuchang, Hubei Province, is a famous scenic spot. The water is dotted with fishing boats, with towers, terraces, and pavilions around.

东湖位于湖北省武汉市武昌东郊而得名、是武汉市著名的风景区。这里碧波万顷、渔舟荡漾、建有水云乡、听涛轩、行吟阁、长天桥等楼台亭阁、各富景趣。

Yellow Crane Tower, located on the Snake Hill, Hubei Province, was first built in 222, and was destroyed and reconstructed in successive dynasties, until 1988.

　　黄鹤楼位于蛇山黄鹤矶头，楼因山而得名。相传三国吴黄武年间(222)创建，后各代屡毁屡建，仅清朝就重建过四次。清光绪十年(1884)，因附近失火延烧被毁，1988年重建。

Wudang Mountain, also known as Taihe Mountain, is located in Junxian County, Hubei Province. Tianzhu Peak, the highest point, is 1,612 meters above sea level. In 627, the Five-Dragon Memorial Temple was constructed on Lingying Peak, expanded and renovated in the Song and Yuan dynasties and destroyed at the end of the Yuan Dynasty. In 1412, Zhu Di, an emperor of the Ming Dynasty (1368-1644), built a huge Taoist building complex here.

武当山又名太和山，在湖北均县境内，是我国名山之一。天柱峰最高，海拔一千六百一十二米，峰奇谷险、洞室幽邃。据载，唐太宗贞观年间(627)，在灵应峰创建五龙祠，宋、元以来，增修扩建，元末毁于战火。明成祖朱棣 即位后，于永乐十年(1412)，命工部侍郎郭进率三十万人，在此大兴土木，建成了庞大的道教建筑群。故有"五里一庵十里宫、丹墙翠瓦望玲珑"之说，概括了武当山建筑规模的宏伟。

Xiling Gorge, located in Yichang County, Hubei Province, is the longest of the three famous gorges on the Yangtze River. The zigzagging river, the reefs and the swift currents form a beautiful landscape.

西陵峡位于宜昌县南津关，是长江三峡中最长的峡谷。水流回环曲折、江中礁石林立、险滩密布、水势湍急、云雾升腾、气象万千，好似一幅精美的山水画。

Hunan Province is located on the middle reaches of the Yangtze River, south of Dongting Lake. It is known for its many scenic spots, including Yuelu Mountain, Orange Island, Dongting Lake, Zhangjiajie Nature Reserve, Yueyang Tower, and Jiuyi Mountain. Mount Hengshan, in the center of the province, is one of the five famous mountains in China, with lofty peaks, tall trees, beautiful flowers and exotic plants, serving as an ideal summer resort.

湖南省位于长江中游、洞庭湖以南。岳麓 山、橘子洲、洞庭湖、张家界、岳阳楼、九疑山，都是湖南省的重要景区。位于湖南省中部的衡山，是著名的中国五岳之一，山势雄伟，古木参天，奇花异草，四时郁香，是游览避暑的好地方。

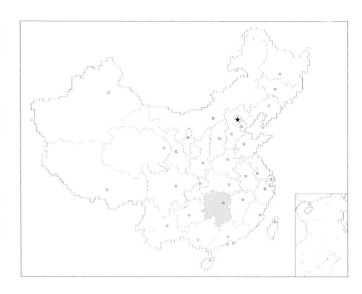

Shaoshan Hill, located in Xiangtan County, Hunan Province, is the hometown of Mao Zedong, former chairman of the People's Republic of China. It is one of the 72 peaks of the Mount Hengshan.

韶山位于湖南省湘潭县境内，是毛泽东的故乡。此处峰峦耸峙，气势磅礴，是南岳七十二峰之一。韶山冲群山环抱，松柏葱茏，风景极为秀丽。

Mount Hengshan is famous for its old pine trees and varieties of flowers.

衡山古松是南岳的象征，山上古木参天，山下四季花香。有红花油茶、日本樱花、毛皂荚、猕猴脆桃等。珍贵植物，种类繁多。

Mount Hengshan, located in the middle of Hunan Province, is one of the five famous mountains in China with beautiful scenery in all four seasons.

衡山属中国五岳之一、古称南岳，位于湖南省中部。这里风景绚丽多彩，四季飞云流雾、时而波涛汹涌、时而风平浪静、素有五岳独秀之美称。

Zhangjiajie Nature Reserve, located to the north of Dayong City, Hunan Province, composes the Wulingyuan Scenic Zone, together with Suoxiyu Valley and Tianzi Hill, with exotic peaks.

张家界位于湖南省西部的大庸市北部，它东与索溪峪相接，北与天子山相邻形成武灵源风景区。张家界奇峰林立，形态各异，有的像金鞭，笔架，有的像猿猴，苍鹰，是一处特色鲜明的原始景观。

Tianzi Hill is a newly discovered scenic spot with karst topography.

　　天子山亦属岩溶地貌，山间万木葱茏，谷下清水潺潺，形成了各种奇特的景观，是我国新兴的重要风景区。

Huang's Family Village gives a panoramic view of Wulingyuan Nature Reserve.

　　黄氏寨的自然风景，是其他各地所罕见。登临黄氏寨，可以俯瞰武灵源全景，群峰矗立，拔地而起，云雾缭绕、忽明忽暗，是不可多得的自然景观。

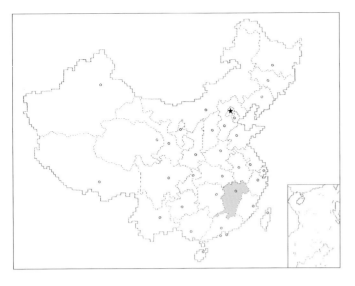

Jiangxi Province is located in the southwest of Central East China to the south of the Yangtze River. Famous natural sceneries include Hundred-Flower Islet, King Teng's Pavilion, Jinggang Hill, Smoky Water Pavilion, Boyang Lake and White Egret Island. In addition, beautiful Mount Lushan has long been a particular attraction.

江西省位于中国华东地区西南部，长江中下游南岸。这里的著名风景有百花洲、滕王阁、井冈山、烟水亭、鄱阳湖、白鹭洲，以及湖光山色，妙趣横生的庐山风光。均已成为劳动人民疗养和游览的胜地，也是国际友人向往的地方。

Baihua (Hundred Flowers) Islet, located on the East Lake of Nanchang City, Jiangxi Province, became a tourist destination after a bridge and a pavilion were built.

百花洲在江西省南昌市状元桥和三道桥之间的东湖一带。共有三洲，其中两洲在八一公园内，一洲为省图书馆旁。原为水泽之乡，潆回环抱。南宋绍兴(1131-1163)年间，豫章节度使张澄在此建讲武亭以习水军。解放后，东湖几经疏没，在湖中筑岛修堤，架桥建亭，成为游览胜地。

King Teng's Tower, located by the Ganjiang River at Nanchang, Jiangxi Province, was constructed by Li Yuanying, younger brother of Li Shimin, the second emperor of the Tang Dynasty. The tower was then destroyed and reconstructed 28 times. The latest reconstruction was in 1990.

滕王阁位于南昌市沿江路赣江边。唐永徽四年(653)，太宗李世民之弟、滕王李元婴都督洪州时营建，阁以其封号命名。在历时一千三百多年中，屡毁屡建，重建重修约二十八次，1926 年被北洋军阀邓如琢绕毁，1990 年重建。

Smoky Water Pavilion, located in Gantang Lake in Jiujiang, Jiangxi Province, was built between 816 and 818. It is connected with Zhou Yu, a general of the Three Kingdoms Period (220-280). The pavilion was built by Bai Juyi, a Tang Dynasty poet, when he was in exile in Jiangzhou. The scenic spots include Chunyang Hall, Cuizhao Hall, Wuxian Tower and Jingbo Tower.

烟水亭位于九江市甘棠湖中，建于唐元和十一至十三年(816-818)。相传为三国时东吴都督周瑜点将台旧址。唐诗人白居易贬为江州司马时，建亭于其上。现有纯阳殿、翠照轩、五贤阁、宴会厅、境波楼等。为九江旅游胜地。

Mount Lushan, located to the south of Jiujiang, Jiangxi Province, is by the Yangtze River and Poyang Lake. It is said that seven brothers of the Kuang family during the Zhou Dynasty lived as hermits in thatched huts on the mountain. The scenic spots include Fairy Cave, Wulao Peak, Dragon Head Cliff, Big Heavenly Pool, and White Deer Cave.

庐山在九江市南，飞峙长江边，紧靠鄱阳湖。相传周朝有匡氏七兄弟上山修道，草庐为舍，故称匡庐。其中仙人洞、五老峰、龙首崖、含鄱口、大天池、白鹿洞等，四季风景如画，夏季凉爽宜人。

Stone Bell Hill is located at the entrance to Poyang Lake, Hukou County. Upper Stone Bell Mountain is in the south, and Lower Stone Bell Mountain is in the north. The name derives from the sound of waves from the lake echoing in caves under the mountain. The scenic spots include Half-Mountain Pavilion, Huaisu Pavilion and Huanxiang Villa, all built in the Qing Dynasty (1644-1911).

石钟山位于湖口县鄱阳湖入口处。南为上石钟山、北为下石钟山，山下有洞，浪击洞中声若宏钟，故得此名。这里湖光山色，风景宜人，山上从唐代就有建筑，几经兴废。半山亭、怀素亭、极慈禅林、浣香别墅等，均为清代所建。

Jinggang Mountain, located on the border between Jiangxi and Hunan provinces, became the first rural revolutionary base in China in October 1927, when Mao Zedong set it up.

井冈山位于江西湖南两者交界处，罗宵山脉中段。井冈山拔地而起，山势雄伟险峻。1927年10月，毛泽东率领秋收起义部队挺进井冈山，创立了全国第一个农村革命根据地。

Heilongjiang Province is located in the far northeast of China, bordering Russia in the north and east. Sun Island, Mirror Lake, Xinglong Temple and the Underground Forest are beautiful scenic attractions here. An ice sculpture exhibition is held here every year, attracting thousands of tourists from both at home and abroad.

黑龙江省位于中国东北地区最北部、北面和东面与俄罗斯为邻。太阳岛、镜泊湖、兴隆寺、地下森林，都是这里的美丽风景。其中一年一度的冰雕艺术展都在这里举行，吸引了无数国际友人。

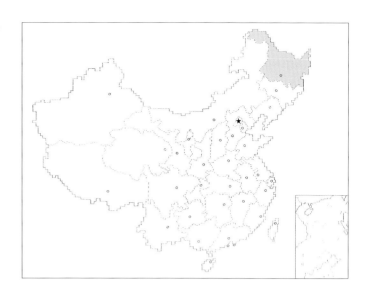

Ice lanterns are a special art in Harbin, capital of Heilongjiang Province. Every winter, an ice lantern festival is held here, with exhibits carved by artists from all over the world.

冰灯是黑龙江省哈尔滨市的独特艺术。每年冬季冰灯艺术节在这里举行，展示雕刻艺术家的作品。如今，许多国际友人也到这里参加冰灯制作。每年春节前后来这里参观冰灯艺术的游客很多。

Mirror Lake is located in the south of Ning'an County, Heilongjiang Province. The water is shallow in the south and deep in the north, with the shallowest point being one meter, and the deepest 60 meters. The eight scenic spots on the lake include Big Fox Hill, Small Fox Hill and Pearl Gate.

镜泊湖位于黑龙江省安宁县南部，湖狭长形约四十五公里。湖水南浅北深，最浅处约一米左右，深处达六十余米。两岸群峰起伏，林木丛生，湖中有大孤山、小孤山、珍珠门等八大奇观。

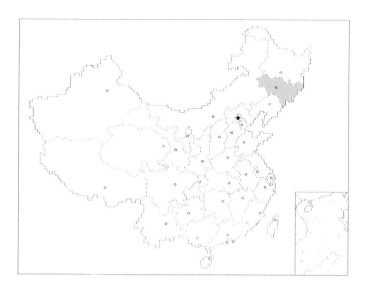

Jilin Province is located in the center of Northeast China, facing Korea across the river in the northeast and bordering Russia in the east. Famous places of historical interest include Taiwang Tomb, Capital Tomb, Huaiyuan Tower, Songhua Lake and the Changbai Mountains Nature Reserve.

　　吉林省位于中国东北地区的中部，东南部与朝鲜隔江相望，东部与俄罗斯接壤。这里著名的文物古迹有太王墓、将军坟、怀远楼、松花湖、以及长白山自然保护区等。长白山是我国最大的自然保护区之一，自然环境和生态系统完整，生物种源丰富。

Trees covered with rime are special scenes in Jilin City, capital of Jilin Province. When winter comes, all the trees are covered by ice and snow, from vapor that arises from the part of the Songhua River that passes the Fengman Hydropower Station.

　　吉林树桂是吉林市的一大美景，每逢冬季到处呈现出银枝冰花，恰似仙境。因吉林市地处松花江畔，江水通过严冬而不固的丰满水电站时，水气蒸腾，遇风寒冻结，便形成一个银色世界。游人到此，心旷神怡。

Heavenly Lake in the Changbai Mountains is located at the top of Baitou Hill, the major peak. There are 16 exotic peaks around the typical highland lake, which is 2,155 meters above sea level.

长白山天池位于长白山主峰白头山顶。池周奇峰十六座，在群山怀抱中有一火山口，汇泉黛碧，名曰天池。海拔二千一百五十五米，是典型的高山湖泊。

144

The 68-meter-high waterfall in the Changbai Mountains originates in Heavenly Lake.

长白山瀑布源于白头山天池，池水经闸门而下，形成高达六十八米的长白瀑布。瀑布如白练悬天、凌空而落，正是"飞流直下三千尺，疑是银河落九天"的壮丽景象。

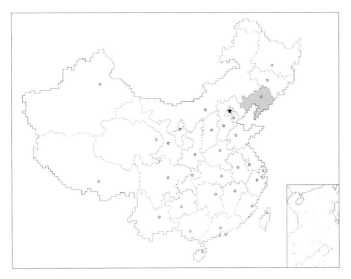

Liaoning Province is located in the south of Northeast China, facing Korea across the river in the east and bordering on the Yellow Sea and the Bohai Sea to the south. Famous scenic spots include Zhaoling Tomb, Fuling Tomb, White Pagoda, Stone Pagoda, Chongxing Temple, Fengguo Temple, and the scenery of Qianshan. The Forbidden City in Shenyang is magnificent, and was modeled after the Forbidden City in Beijing.

辽宁省位于中国东北地区的南部，东面与朝鲜隔江相望，南临黄海和渤海。这里著名的风景区有昭陵、福陵、白塔、石塔、崇兴寺、奉国寺、以及千山风光等。特别是沈阳故宫，楼阁耸立，殿堂巍峨，雕梁画栋，富丽堂皇，是中国现存仅次于北京故宫的最完整的皇宫建筑。

The Forbidden City in Shenyang is located in the center of the old city proper of the capital of Liaoning Province. The first imperial palace of the Qing Dynasty (1644-1911), work started on it in 1625, and was completed in 1636.

沈阳故宫位于沈阳市旧城中心，为清初皇宫。清兵入关后称奉天行宫，清顺治元年(1644)世祖在此即位。始建于后金天命十年(1625)、清崇德元年(1636)基本建成。是我国现存仅次与北京故宫的一座皇宫建筑。

Zhaoling Mausoleum, also known as Northern Mausoleum, located in the north of Shenyang, is the tomb of Emperor Taizong of the Qing Dynasty (1644-1911) and his empress. Construction started in 1643 and ended in 1651. It is the largest and best-preserved tomb among the three mausoleums of the Qing Dynasty outside Beijing.

昭陵又称北陵，位于沈阳市北。是清太宗皇太极和孝端文皇后博尔济吉特氏的陵墓。建于清崇德八年(1643)年，竣工于顺治八年(1651)。是关外清代三陵中规模最大、最完整的一座。崇楼大殿掩映在苍松翠柏之间，风景十分幽美。

Mount Qianshan (Thousand Hills), located in the east ▷ of Anshan City, Liaoning Province, is one of the three famous mountains in the northeast area. There are 999 peaks, hence the name. The highest ones are Fairy Terrace and Five-Buddha Peak.

千山位于辽宁省鞍山市东，是东北地区三大名山之一。山中奇峰迭起，塔寺棋布、共有峰峦九百九十九座，以其近千，故名千山。最高峰是仙人台和五佛顶，有五大禅林、十二观，皆掩映在重峦茂林之中。

Bihai (Blue Aea) Villa is located in the northeast of Tiger Beach in Dalian, Liaoning Province. There is a bathing beach in the north, and a seaside park in the south. It attracts tourists from both at home and abroad every year with its beautiful environment, and convenient accommodation and transportation.

碧海山庄是大连市改革开放后的一处新型建筑，位于老虎滩东北方向的 海滩上。山庄北有海滨浴场，南有海滨公园，这里食宿洁净，交通方便，旅游旺季中外游人络绎不绝。

Map Index

图 版 目 录

图书在版编目（CIP）数据

漫游神州／孙永学编辑撰文；刘春根等摄影．－北京：外文出版社，2001
ISBN 7-119-02158-3

Ⅰ．漫…Ⅱ．①孙…②刘…Ⅲ．名胜古迹－中国－摄影集 Ⅳ．K928.7-64
中国版本图书馆 CIP 数据核字(97)第 27247 号

Editor: Sun Yongxue
Executive Editor: Zhou Daguang
Front Cover Designer: Zhou Daguang and Wu Tao
Layout Designer: Zhou Daguang and Zhu Zhen'an
Translator: Ren Ying
Language Consultant: Paul White
Photographers: Sun Yongxue, Liu Chungen et al.

编　撰: 孙永学
责　编: 周大光
封面设计: 周大光　吴　涛
内页设计: 周大光　朱振安
翻　译: 任　瑛
英文改稿: 保罗·怀特
摄　影: 孙永学　刘春根等

First Edition 2001

Touring China

ISBN 7-119-02158-3

© Foreign Languages Press
Published by Foreign Languages Press
24 Baiwanzhuang Road, Beijing 100037, China
Home Page: http://www.flp.com.cn
E-mail Addresses: info @ flp.com.cn
　　　　　　　　sales @ flp.com.cn
Printed in the People's Republic of China

漫游神州

孙永学　编撰

©　外文出版社
外文出版社出版
（中国北京百万庄大街 24 号）
邮政编码：　100037
外文出版社网页：http://www.flp.com.cn
外文出版社电子邮件地址：info @ flp.com.cn
　　　　　　　　　　　　sales @ flp.com.cn
北京骏马行图文中心制版
天时印刷（深圳）有限公司印刷
2001 年(竖 12 开)第一版
2001 年第一版第一次印刷
ISBN 7-119-02158-3/J·1414（外）
12800（平）